God,
Suffering,
&
Belief

HOWARD R. BURKLE

God,
Suffering,
&
Belief

ABINGDON   NASHVILLE

God, Suffering, and Belief

Copyright © 1977 by Abingdon

Library of Congress Cataloging in Publication Data

BURKLE, HOWARD R
  God, suffering, and belief.
  Includes index.
  1. Suffering. I. Title.
BT732.7.B78   248'.3   76-26496

ISBN 0-687-15446-4

MANUFACTURED BY THE PARTHENON PRESS AT
NASHVILLE, TENNESSEE, UNITED STATES OF AMERICA

To Anita & Ken,
Crystal & Howard

PREFACE

I wish to express my gratitude to Grinnell College for a faculty research grant that provided a stimulating period of summer study in New York City. During this sojourn I carried out the initial reading, reflection, and outlining from which this book has grown. I wish to thank Grinnell College also for underwriting the preparation of the typescript. These palpable expressions of help and confidence greatly increased the satisfaction and lessened the tedium of the writing process.

I wish also to thank Heidi Burkle, Amy Burkle, Jeanne Burkle, Carol Vogt, and Nancy Ganschaw for help with the typing; Harold Kasimow for his sensitive and encouraging critique of chapter 2; William R. Jones for his extraordinarily careful and acute analysis of chapter 3; Theodore M. McConnell for his evaluation of the whole manuscript and for wise guidance about publication; Lynne Fitch for her suggestions on the importance of avoiding sexist language; and Jeanne Burkle for her reinforcement of the sexist language issue and for her patient insistence on the indispensability of women's experience to any realistic treatment of the problem of suffering. Without all of this help and the stimulation of my students and faculty colleagues at Grinnell, I could not have carried through my project.

Howard Burkle
Grinnell, Iowa

CONTENTS

INTRODUCTION

Is it possible to believe in God in spite of the "absurdity" seemingly endemic to the human situation? By "absurdity" I mean any aspect of human experience which seems clearly inappropriate and incongruous in a world governed by the just and loving God of the Bible. This book answers this question affirmatively; moreover, by confronting the most severe forms of absurdity—cosmic abandonment, genocide, racism, and sexism—it tries to demonstrate that one can believe without lapsing into irrationality. My hope is that the argument which follows shows that believing in God is not inconsistent with the lamentable fact that humanity suffers and that it sometimes suffers cruelly and unjustly. I wish, too, to affirm that no one need be ashamed of believing in God. Believing is neither an intellectual disgrace nor, on the other hand, proof of sanctity; it is a legitimate, honorable, and exceedingly difficult project.

When I utter the constantly invoked, incorrigibly ambiguous word "God," I am thinking in basically traditional terms—that is, of a definite, personal existent who transcends yet directly relates to the world which it creates. I do not mean to be more specifically traditional than this; I am not espousing the God formulated by Augustine, Aquinas, Luther, Calvin, or Barth. In fact, there are many facets of these mainstream Christian concepts of God which I reject and would like to see corrected by insights drawn from current process theology. As will be evident, my suggestions for dealing with the problems of absurdity owe a great deal to the doctrine of divine relativity set forth by Charles Hartshorne and others who have followed his lead.

When I confess to being traditional, I am acknowledging ideas of God which are more biblical, more concretely religious, and, some will think, more naïve than those of classical theistic metaphysics. The God I think we are entitled to believe in is the deity of the New Testament, the Heavenly Parent of Jesus Christ. Of course, there is no end of controversy about this deity, not only as to how it should be conceived but even as to whether it is anything more than a mythical fiction of the prescientific era. However, I do not wish to involve this discussion in those difficult issues; the issues we shall tackle are difficult enough in their own right. I shall use "God" to designate the supposed Creator, Redeemer, and Sanctifier of the world, the Eternal Person who exists independently of the creation yet participates by power in the processes of nature and by persuasive presence in human history. It seems clear enough that Jesus and the early disciples believed in such a God, whether or not we decide to do so.

I deliberately say "Parent" rather than "Father" and "it" rather than "he" in the paragraphs above because I am convinced that it is vital that we break the idolatrous identification of maleness with deity which flaws Christianity and the other religions which stem from the Hebrew Bible. As I shall argue, this unwarranted deification of maleness and the correlative depreciation of femaleness is the underlying cause of the most ancient, widespread, and debilitating of all the forms of human suffering—the suppression of women. Consequently, I shall not, *except* when quoting, paraphrasing, or representing the thought of someone else who does refer to God in sexual terms, use sexual words to refer to God or to human beings generically. The resulting terminology ("it" instead of "he" for pronominal references to God and "humanity" and "humankind" instead of "man" and "mankind" for human beings) may seem awkward at first but should grow less so as it becomes familiar.

There are those, like English theologian Alistair Kee, who say that *choosing* to believe in God is impossible because what people believe is first of all fixed by cultural conditioning; and since Western culture today is secular-atheistic, none living within its sphere of influence can believe in God.[1] I do not accept this. Surely human powers of deliberation and execution are not so passive as this. If we look at what people actually do rather than what some *a priori* theory on the interrelation of society and thought says they ought to do, we shall find that people are able to change their minds about believing and disbelieving. What I observe in the people around me—those I sit with in church and chat with at the grocery, my family, students, friends, colleagues, and fellow citizens—is basically what I have seen for as long as I have been sensitive to this issue: some people believe in God, some do not; some are ardent, others casual; some are convinced, some uncertain; some are sincere, others hypocritical. The situation is exceedingly mixed and fluid, but it is not stagnant or dominated by unbelief, and it does not seem to be wholly determined by massive societal forces.

There are others who say that believing in God is an anachronism. Theologian Thomas Altizer, for instance, maintains that contemporary secular culture "is a world which has wholly detached itself from the traditional faith of Christendom."[2] I do not accept this either. No doubt there are some who consider believing in God inconsistent with their contemporary "scientific" world view, and their numbers may be growing. However, the situation is not nearly so bleak as Altizer alleges. Sociologist A. M. Greeley finds that there has been "almost no change . . . in the religious attitude and behavior of American gentiles between 1952 and 1965."[3] More recently [1974], Robert Wuthnow and Charles Y. Glock have found much the same thing. Compared with their parents, people today attend church less often and are less orthodox in how they think of God, but they believe just as much in God, the efficacy of prayer, and the afterlife. The evidence is that "three respondents in four believe in some concept of the supernatural."[4] If any alarm should be raised over the state of religious belief, it is not that too few people believe at all, but that too many believe thoughtlessly and automatically. If any charge should be brought against believers, it is that we presume to believe without coming to grips with the harsh realities of human suffering.

My intention here is not to deny that people today find belief difficult, but to deny exaggerated conceptions of the difficulty. We should resist no less the handful of despairing theologians who tell us that belief is futile than the legion of zealous apologists who assure us that we may believe without profound soul-searching. Against the former I shall defend the rationality of belief, and against the latter I shall insist on our earning the right to believe.

I do not deny that believing in God these days may be more difficult than it has ever been before. There are certainly signs of this. In the religious permissiveness of secular society, the onus of decision is on the individual. Ideally, people are considered to be free, potentially mature agents who are expected to make up their own minds and bear the uncertainties of responsible commitment. Moreover, religious choice is made more difficult by the immense and bewildering increase in the amount of information available about the universe. Every advance in scientific knowledge seems to deepen the ethical and theological mystery. Also, our situation is complicated by the fact that in an age of rapid transportation and instant communication we are exposed, as never before, to the religious views of other cultures. Their beliefs impinge on ours as troubling alternatives or as rival claimants for loyalty.

Of all the factors which make belief difficult for moderns, however, the most important is human suffering. For obvious reasons, suffering has always posed a special difficulty for those who believe or wish to believe in God. Today, suffering seems even more difficult to reconcile with God. Because of the electronic media, we have almost instantaneous access to information about the condition of humankind everywhere. Our horizons of awareness are wider and more filled with details, and we are compelled to adjust to conditions of misery which our forebears could simply ignore. We know, however adroitly we block it from awareness, that at any given moment a sizable portion of the human race is in agony.

Another reason the problem of evil seems so theologically troublesome today is that because of technological advances, suffering takes place on a larger scale than ever before. Wars are fought worldwide. Hunger jeopardizes whole peoples. Nuclear and biological weapons and over-population threaten the entire race. Today's suffering is not merely local tragedy but global catastrophe.

We shall consider the four forms of suffering—the "faces of absurdity," we might call them—which seem to pose the greatest threat to belief in God. Some persons today see all humanity as *abandoned* in a spiritually empty, purposeless, and ultimately destructive universe. Others are stunned because God seems to have *betrayed* its people into the hands of genocidal murderers. There are others who think that perhaps God *hates* their racial group and has locked them within a social system dominated by racist oppressors. There are others who say the Father God regards women as inferior to men and sanctions women's *suppression*.

Whether we can confront all the faces of absurdity and still feel justified in believing in God remains to be seen. Abandonment we can deal with well enough, I think. It is the absurdities of religious genocide, racism, and sexism which are most threatening to belief. Theologians have neglected them—fled from them, actually. We have not come to terms with the murder of the Jews and the oppression of blacks and women, and I doubt that we can do so successfully without giving up certain venerable assumptions about what God does in the world.

One person who has not failed to face absurdity is British philosopher Alasdair MacIntyre. In 1967 he reviewed Ulrich Simon's *Theology of Auschwitz,* which portrays the Nazi death camps as nothing less than hell on earth. The murder and torture perpetrated by the Nazis were not only vast in number but unsurpassed in wickedness. They were deliberate and sprang from an unlimited will to destroy. The camps, Simon declares, were the worst of all possible worlds, so horrible that not even divine love can forgive those who made them. Hell is too good for the creators of Auschwitz. Hitler and his accomplices are utterly unredeemable.

MacIntyre accepts Simon's prophecies and says that anyone who claims to be a Christian should speak out and agree with him. The murderers of Auschwitz must not be forgiven. Then MacIntyre takes a step beyond Simon. He includes God with Hitler.

What I am inclined to do is to offer an alternative and rival religious affirmation: if there is an eternal God who stood by while

Auschwitz happened and did nothing to prevent it, then do not let him set himself up before us on the Day of Judgment. Above all let us have no divine cant about his forgiving us our sins. It will be God who will need to be forgiven.[5]

God, like Hitler, is beyond forgiveness. What is needed, MacIntyre insists, is not prayer, nor laughter, nor tears, and certainly not what he calls "a flight to theology." What is needed is a real effort to understand what happened at Auschwitz.

That we need to understand Auschwitz there is no doubt, but that theology will lead us away from reality is not necessarily true. Actually there can be no profound understanding of Auschwitz unless we do probe the theological implications of that staggering tragedy. MacIntyre's own dramatic assertion that God needs our forgiveness cries out for explanation, and his decision to reject God is highly significant theologically, especially when viewed against the background of his earlier, more traditional stand on the problem of evil. In 1959 he wrote an acute little book called *Difficulties in Christian Belief,* which focuses on the problem of evil as the chief obstacle to believing in God. The problem arises, MacIntyre says, from the logical inconsistency among the three statements "God is omnipotent," "God is wholly good," and "Evils occur in the universe."[6] He examines five standard solutions having to do with evil which are sometimes thought to remove the inconsistency: (1) evil is punishment, (2) evil is discipline, (3) evil is education, (4) evil is a consequence of free will, and (5) evil is mystery. MacIntyre weighs each of these possibilities and concludes that they all fail.[7]

Then he considers a sixth possibility, that evil occurs because God has created the world as a place for self-determining agents to exercise responsible choices. God wishes human beings to be capable of moral failure and of refusing to grow. Thus, God wills that the world be a place where both good and evil are possible, and although he does not desire evil, he does in a sense will it. "For God wills that men should do what they will, even if it is not what God would wish them to do."[8]

MacIntyre assesses this argument; and, although he finds it not beyond criticism, he endorses it. It will serve because, with it, we can "see in outline how the facts of evil have their place in the Christian scheme and how we are not faced by a stark contradiction at this point."[9] At least it provides a basis on which those who already believe in God may continue to do so without involving themselves in sheer irrationality.

MacIntyre's solution is basically the one which I shall affirm and defend in the ensuing discussion. What particularly interests me is that because of the Holocaust MacIntyre finally decides that his solution, too, is inadequate. Less than ten years after the publication of *Difficulties in Christian Belief* he is accusing God of unpardonable treachery and in effect breaking with the Christian faith he had practiced and defended for years. Apparently without any direct knowledge of Rabbi Richard Rubenstein's writings, MacIntyre arrives at the same conclusion which this American-Jewish, so-called radical theologian reaches concerning God—that the horror of the death camps compels us to give up the biblical concept of God as the holy, compassionate Lord of history.

I do not think that MacIntyre is obliged to make this move, but I dare not assert this without looking as carefully and as openly as I can at the absurdities which he and many others think contradict the belief that we are all cared for by a wise and compassionate God. This is what I shall now do.

CHAPTER 1

ABANDONMENT

1. THE SENSE OF ABANDONMENT

In a widely read essay defining and defending his brand of existentialism, philosopher Jean-Paul Sartre says: "When we speak of 'abandonment' . . . we only mean to say that God does not exist, . . . and man is in consequence forlorn, for he cannot find anything to depend upon either within or outside himself."[1] The sense of cosmic aloneness expressed here is not simply the despairing plaint of an eccentric philosophy called existentialism. A wide spectrum of thinkers—some of them eminent defenders of belief in God—are convinced that most people today live without a sense of God's presence. Martin Buber declares that in our time God is in "eclipse." Dietrich Bonhoeffer says that this is a "post-Christian period," and Alistair Kee terms it a "post-religious era." Theodore Roszak describes Christian-scientific culture as a "spiritual wasteland."

Abandonment is not only the absence of belief; it is a condition of profound spiritual emptiness. Catholic philosopher Michael Novak calls this the "experience of nothingness," "an experience beyond the limits of reason. It arises near the borderline of insanity. It is terrifying. It makes all attempts at speaking of purpose . . . seem doubtful and spurious."[2] Novak confesses to having felt this terrifying emptiness in his own life and suggests that it troubles virtually everyone in Western society. Boredom, anomie, social permissiveness, helplessness, and drug abuse, he says, are some of its more obvious symptoms.

Not everyone admits to such feelings of desperate spiritual isolation, and those who do may not attribute them to the absence of God. Nevertheless, according to many of our foremost theologians, these feelings are pervasive and profound. Moreover, given the world in which we live, it could not be otherwise. Underlying our technologically formed society there is a "culturally innate" world view which asserts that nature stands alone, exists in its own right, and can be understood without reference to anything beyond itself. Although this ideology, which is generally called "secularism," does not necessarily explicitly deny God, it does exclude God from serious concern and thus treat God as irrelevant.[3]

Whether or not they think about God, persons who base their lives on these cultural postulates have made themselves vulnerable to the condition of abandonment. They need only some social trauma or personal tragedy to bring to the center of awareness what has been at the periphery all along. In the vastness of space and the limitless flow of time they are alone. Suddenly they begin to feel their nothingness—not the traditional nothingness of the creature shuddering before the majesty of the Creator but the nothingness of insignificant *homo sapiens* shivering before the cold impersonality of the universe. Although written forty years ago, these words by historian Carl Becker express the secular mood of today precisely.

> What is man that the electron should be mindful of him? Man is but a foundling in the cosmos, abandoned by the forces that created him. Unparented, unassisted and undirected by omniscient or benevolent authority, he must fend for himself, and with the aid of his own limited intelligence find his way about in an indifferent universe.[4]

Along with the indifference of the world goes a sense of purposelessness. Human history does not flow toward a meaningful goal; the living forms on this planet seem to have no reason for existing; the vast inanimate world gives no evidence of having been deliberately created. The world presents itself as a vast collection of mystifying stellar systems mindlessly pulsing to pointless rhythms. On the planet Earth—and where else, we do not know—life just happens to have emerged. The material potentialities happened to be present and conditions favoring their synthesis happened to prevail. Therefore, life began— spontaneously, accidentally. What is, is, and that is all that can be said about the ultimate origin and destiny of anything. Anyone who presumes to say more than this must assume the burden of proving the need and the right to do so.[5]

I am convinced that the absence of God from the center of our lives, and the intense feeling of abandonment that is latent in this, is one of the salient spiritual maladies of our day. Paul Tillich is surely right that "meaninglessness" is the dominant form of the "threat of nonbeing" in contemporary Western society.[6] People in this society do have extraordinary difficulty living in such a way that God plays a direct and vitalizing role in all they do and feel. Too often even those who say that they believe in God reveal by their timorous and self-preferring behavior that their belief is not rooted in the deep soil of God's presence. If genuineness of belief is measured by the degree to which persons derive the strength and guidance for their daily lives from their relation to God and through God correlate their short-range and self-centered desires with a universally fulfilling global purpose, then belief is indeed rare.

It is possible, of course, to view this atmosphere of divine absence as an auspicious condition. Like German pastor

21

Dietrich Bonhoeffer, we can look on this "religionless world" as a welcome opportunity to grow up spiritually and learn to live without undue dependence on God. Like the Dutch theologian Cornelius van Peursen, we can regard secularization as a liberating stage in history which frees human beings from a mythological relation to nature. Like American theologian Harvey Cox, we can reject the cultural idolatry of secularism and commit ourselves enthusiastically to "secularity," understood as a biblically based, spiritually healthy affirmation of the world as the place where we are to exercise our God-given creativity. I accept all of these positive features of the so-called secular theology. Believing in God should not keep us from accepting the world as our proper place, nor make us afraid to stand erect in reasonable independence of the Creator, nor cause us to wait for God to do for us what we can and should do for ourselves.

However, it is important that we not let our eagerness to live in authentic independence of God obscure the fact that many of our number have lost all association with God. The "withdrawal" of God is not unambiguously benign, not entirely a sign of our "coming of age." For many—and perhaps in some respects, for all of us—it is symptomatic of deep tragedy, of the darkness of the absurdity of radical suffering. As many human beings see it, God has not merely stepped back to give us room to exercise our genius; God has turned away from us. In the venerable Jewish image, we live in a time of the "hiding of the Face."

Of the many thinkers who have written on the subject of abandonment, none is more challenging to those who believe in God than Albert Camus. Camus unequivocally accepts the perspective of abandonment—or "absurdity" as he calls it—as the essential condition of humanity, and with stubborn honesty he analyzes the destructive elements intrinsic to the abandoned situation. Although Camus is also acutely sensitive to the positive features of existence, to the "water, warm stones, and the sea" which his model Sisyphus loves more than the gods, he is particularly perceptive about the negative features: irrationality, injury, sickness, and death. We shall consider the latter as they are portrayed in Camus's last novel, *The Plague*, and his two essays *The Myth of Sisyphus* and *The Rebel*. I am interested in Camus's reasons for thinking that human existence is absurd and in his proposal for living nobly despite the absurdity. I am convinced that no one is entitled to believe in God who has not faced and accounted for the basic negativities with which Camus deals.

2. ABSURDITY IN *THE PLAGUE*

Camus's haunting novel *The Plague* is the story of an epidemic of bubonic plague in the North African city of Oran. On the surface it is just that, the story of death, thousands of agonized deaths, and of the strange reactions which protracted quarantine in a condemned society inspires in the potential next victims, the living. At another level, however, the novel is a richly suggestive exploration of the dimension of absurdity. The epidemic in Oran symbolizes the death and injury which constitute the negative pole of existence as Camus envisions it.

Oran is a comfortable, complacent place that is populated with ordinary, orderly people. During the time of the plague its inhabitants pass through an almost predictable progression of states of mind. At word of the first deaths they are merely curious, then uneasy. As the deaths increase, they become incredulous, panicky, angry, terrified, until finally, deprived of all ability to feel intensely, they settle into a numb indifference. Even before the epidemic has reached its peak of virulence, they learn to look with boredom at the corpses which daily are carried out like garbage and then burned. Under conditions of plague, even death becomes uninteresting.

Among the countless meaningless deaths there are a few which are highly significant both for the story and for anyone who would understand Camus's concept of absurdity. Indeed, these deaths raise the fundamental issues which must be faced by anyone who wishes to believe that human existence is intrinsically meaningful. We must, therefore, reflect upon them carefully.

The first important death is that of a young child, the police magistrate's son. Frail from birth, the child is severely affected by the plague. Nothing Dr. Rieux can do helps much. The child simply passes through the stages of the disease as if the victim of some inexorable sadistic force. Nausea, dizziness, running sores, paralyzing cramps, chills, fierce waves of fever—remorselessly the symptoms follow their path toward the moment of death until, at last, the child lies inert, "racked on the tumbled bed, in a grotesque parody of crucifixion."[7]

Clearly, what Camus is painting is a crucifixion scene: the innocent, unresisting, and deeply pitiable child is sacrificed against his will to some dark determining force. Destroyed before his life has scarcely begun, the child is the epitome of wasted possibility and incompleteness.

Dr. Rieux, the attending physician and the leader of the forces fighting the plague, is so outraged at the child's agony that he undergoes a sort of antireligious conversion. Until that time Rieux had been an unreflecting humanist. He had believed as a matter of course in the intelligibility of nature, the power of science, the goodness of humanity, and the basic justice of human destiny. When the boy dies, however, Rieux is totally shaken, and he turns on Father

Paneloux, the attending priest, and tells him vehemently that he will no longer accept the world. "Until my dying day I shall refuse to love a scheme of things in which children are put to torture!"[8]

This scene contains three of the basic features of Camus's concept of absurdity. First, there is the irrational destructiveness of the world. "Incompleteness" (death) and "wastefulness" (injury) are the omnipresent signs of nature's ineradicable tendency to maim and destroy what it has created.[9] "What's natural is the microbe," a companion of Dr. Rieux's says in a reflective moment.[10] Second, there is the human attitude toward the world. We naturally desire not to be injured and killed. We passionately desire to understand everything, to feel at home, to be happy. Third, there is the human response which arises from the incongruity between our desires and the world. We *feel* strange, alienated, and we *judge* our situation intolerable.

Dr. Rieux's defiant refusal to accept such a world is also an important element of this first death scene, for it suggests the attitude of rebellion, which is Camus's recommended way of dealing with absurdity. We shall consider rebellion shortly, but first it is important to be as precise as possible about absurdity. Strictly speaking, when Camus speaks of absurdity, he is referring to the third feature of absurdity just described. Absurdity involves the destructiveness of the world and humanity's desire to feel perfectly at home, but strictly speaking it is neither of these. It is the combined feeling and judgment which emerges from the clash between these objective and subjective elements. Absurdity is the "unreasonable silence" of the cosmos, excruciatingly assimilated into human conscious-ness. It is humanity's infinite desire to know, lying broken at the foot of the "walls of irrationality" which it has futilely tried to surmount. Absurdity is the darkness in which we are aware that we are alone, unknown, and unwelcome.[11]

The second of the significant deaths is that of Father Paneloux, referred to already as the priest in attendance at the death of the child. Paneloux is a curious figure, difficult to characterize because he undergoes considerable change in the course of the novel. In the beginning he is the archtraditionalist—indeed, a caricature of a traditionalist. Soon after the plague takes hold and at last is openly acknowledged as an epidemic, Paneloux preaches a sermon that is a gem of vindictiveness and insensitivity. He pompously announces to the large, frightened congregation that the plague is God's punishment for their wickedness, and he warns them that the destruction will not cease until they have repented for their failure to love God enough—by which he means chiefly their laxity in attending Mass. Arrogant, shallow, censorious, Paneloux is everything a Christian should not be but, ironically, precisely what Camus thinks the typical Christian is.

As the plague continues month after month, slaying the virtuous as well as the wicked, Paneloux begins to waver in his traditionalist interpretation and after the death of the little boy, he delivers a second sermon in which he abandons his belief that the plague is divine justice. Saying "we," rather than "you" as he had in the first sermon, Paneloux speculates that the plague may be God's way of deepening spirituality. His dogmatism now gone, Paneloux does not claim to know that what he is saying is true. He stands before the people less as a preacher than as a fellow sufferer. He is a living instance of his own new theory that suffering deepens spirituality, for certainly he has been humbled and humanized. At the climax of his sermon he suggests that perhaps the chief duty of Christians in times of suffering is to love what they cannot understand.

In his death, which follows shortly after this sermon,

Paneloux is true to this new conviction. Afflicted with a plaguelike ailment, he isolates himself in his bedroom and forbids his housekeeper to call a physician because he thinks that such stoicism is what those who truly believe that suffering is spiritual testing must display. They must embrace whatever befalls them as God's will. They must be prepared to love even death. Therefore Paneloux lies quietly, resigned and uncomplaining, clutching his crucifix to his breast. The housekeeper watches bewildered as he rebuffs her efforts to help. Dr. Rieux, whom the house-keeper calls in only just before Paneloux's death, studies the symptoms curiously, gazes down upon the posture of grim submission, and declares it "a dubious case."

Paneloux's response is, thus, precisely the opposite of Rieux's. While Rieux refuses to accept a scheme which puts children to torture, Paneloux tries with all his weakened power to love it. One hates death and fights against it; the other loves death and submits to it. One finds the plague incomprehensible; the other, uncomprehend-ingly, accepts it as part of God's transcendent wisdom.

The third significant death is that of the enigmatic Tarrou, a visitor to Oran whose occupation at first seems to be nothing more than observing the people around him and attempting to become a "saint without God." Tarrou is a fascinating character and is, I think, an example of what Camus considers the most adequate and noblest attitude toward absurdity. Tarrou's nature is most veiled at the outset. He appears here and there noting the spread of the disease and raising questions about its meaning. He is one of the first to notice the sickness of the rats and to point out its dangerous potential for infecting the human population. Tarrou is a kind of expert on death. His mission is to be alert to the threat of death and by example to encourage others to be alert and thoughtful.

Tarrou also shows a marked preference for odd persons—the old man who does nothing all day except spit at cats and the bedridden asthmatic who passes his time counting and recounting his bowl of peas. These persons, Tarrou muses, "must be saints."

These curious attitudes of Tarrou's appear as more than mere eccentricities only after Tarrou's past is partially revealed in an intimate conversation with his close friend Dr. Rieux. Prior to his exile in Oran, Tarrou had lived through a complicated series of personal projects which show that he is, in Camus's terms, a "rebel." At only seventeen years he had an experience which prompted him to reject the world. What Dr. Rieux discovered at maturity by the bed of the dying child, Tarrou discovered as a juvenile one day while watching his father, a prominent lawyer, argue a case in court. The father was prosecuting some unfortunate man and arguing for the death penalty when it suddenly struck Tarrou that his father, with his red robes of justice and smooth oratory, symbolized the quintessential shame of human society, namely, that it is based on death. In its customs, morality, and laws, society legitimates and honors killing. It could not survive without legalizing death. Police are respected; soldiers are praised; judges are honored. Although in the eyes of society Tarrou's father was skillfully arguing on behalf of justice, in Tarrou's eyes he was urging murder—respectable, civilized, rationalized murder. In a spontaneous decision the youth resolved to say no to death and yes to life. He left the courtroom at once and soon after ran away from home, never to return.

Tarrou's first act of rebellion was directed against society, Rieux's against nature. Camus calls the former "revolution" because it struggles to purge death from human institutions. He calls the other "metaphysical rebellion" because it is an effort within a person's own thinking to oppose the death forces built into the universe itself.[12] As a rebel, Rieux does what he can to moderate the destructivity of nature; he fights death ("Death and disease is what I hate," he tells Tarrou), and he alleviates pain whenever he can. However, he knows that he can do nothing to change the basic structure of the universe. All he controls is his own attitude, which he changes. Never again will he feel at home in this world or think that it is ordered toward human well-being.

Tarrou, on the other hand, rebels by trying to reform society. After leaving home, he joins a revolutionary group and for a time works at overthrowing governments; but soon he realizes that his fellow revolutionaries are as prepared to kill their enemies as any "establishment" power. Thereupon, he decides that revolutionary societies are ethically no different from those they seek to change, and he rejects revolution.

It is soon after this that Tarrou comes to Oran and commences his search for "sainthood." Now unalterably pacific and committed to life, he is determined to do nothing to collaborate with the forces of death. For himself, he seeks "comprehension" and "tranquillity." He is interested in everyone and everything around him. He is particularly fond of Dr. Rieux and joins him in his struggle with the plague. He works tirelessly with the sanitation squads, trying in every way practicable to align himself with life.

Clearly, at this point Tarrou's rebellion has matured into the metaphysical type, for, like Rieux, he is spiritually at war with the destructive undercurrent of nature. Tarrou comes after many years of effort to the mature level of rebellion which Rieux reaches in a single stride. At the same time, there is something special about Tarrou's rebellion, something which is hinted at in the brand of sainthood he seeks and which is graphically exhibited in his death. Near the end of the novel (ironically, when the epidemic is almost over), Tarrou becomes ill with a particularly virulent form of plague. The enemy at last puts its hands violently on Tarrou's own being, and the victim immediately shows a new side of himself. He drops his somewhat theoretical, contemplative manner and throws his total energy into action.

It is more than simply a struggle to stay alive, more even than defiance of the archmanifestation of evil. It is a display of human indomitability, of heroism that goes beyond mere courage. Once again, we have a crucifixion scene, but now with an aura of victory. Unlike the helpless child and the supine Paneloux, Tarrou fights. He will not willingly give an inch. To every assault of death he responds with the counterforce of life. Above all, he battles to remain conscious, to look steadily and searchingly at everything that is happening. Comprehension is his goal—to illuminate the darkness of death with the light of human understanding. He is never bitter, and although he suffers, he never loses control. To the end, he never ceases fighting. Finally, with a cry, he yields and dies, a smile on his lips. In death he finds peace, not in dying itself, but in his way of dying. Presumably he gains what he has been seeking: sainthood.

3. THE EXTREMITY OF CAMUS'S VISION

Now that the meaning of absurdism is before us, we can raise some questions concerning its adequacy. Is Camus right that we are locked in a hostile embrace with the world?[13] What is the evidence? I think Camus would reply that the evidence is precisely what we have been discussing: the murderous thrust of nature and human society. The world contains not only natural beauty and human nobility, but the twin evils of death and suffering, which ultimately control our fate. It should be plain to all who are honest that the world is fundamentally structured not only to nurture but to injure and, finally, destroy us. [14]

Of course, there is a measure of truth in this: no human being lives untouched by tragedy, and eventually everyone dies. However, surely this is not enough evidence to establish that existence is *absurd*. Are there not cogent reasons why human beings are vulnerable to injury and death? And do not beauty and life rank with injury and death as co-determinants of the meaning of existence? Why does Camus, who is keenly aware of all this, subordinate the positive elements to the negative? Why does he not conclude, as the evidence suggests, that the world is a place of mixed effect, sometimes helpful and sometimes disruptive? Why does he not decide that the world is challenging, puzzling, or mysterious, instead of absurd?

One reason Camus cannot accept this moderate position is his grandiose idea of human nature. He takes as an axiom, that human beings *ought* to be totally exempt from injury and death.[15] Therefore, the very fact that we are hurt and that we eventually die is in itself proof of the unsuitability of existence. Here we have our "Cartesian" starting point, the root certainty to which everyone who does not "cheat" must absolutely hold: existence is absurd. Existence gives us much that is supportive and lovely, and it is precious; but attending all that pleases us are the inescapable adversaries which ultimately negate us. Given such a notion of humanity's due and destiny, it is not difficult to understand Camus's melancholic estimate of our situation.

What is the source of this exalted idea of human entitlement, and why should it govern human thinking? Indeed, what right has Camus, who denies God and transcendent moral standards, to make any statement about

31

what ought to be? Here we must follow what Camus calls the "absurdist logic." Paradoxically, it is *because* (as he thinks) there is no God and no independent moral norms that human beings can make ultimately valid declarations about what ought to be. When the world does not value us, we become free to value ourselves. When the world assaults us, we act. We decide not to accept indifference and murderous hostility. We "rebel." As we do so, we discover that there is reason to value ourselves, that we *are* beings of extraordinary worth. We do not merely decree that we are of value; we discover that we *are* so.[16]

The reason our situation is absurd, therefore, is that in the final accounting the world does not confirm our deepest instincts and judgments about our own significance. Human beings desire to live and to be *perfectly* at home in the cosmos. Our bodies affirm this automatically. Every heartbeat physically declares that life is good. Moreover, our minds and wills long to concur in the wisdom of the body. We deeply desire to feel and know that life is good. Our minds reach out with an insatiable hunger for life—eternal life—lived forever happily and without the experience of loss or diminution. Since this is what we naturally desire, it is what should be; and since the world is obviously not this way, the world is absurd.

It seems to me that this legislative absoluteness of human desire is, to say the least, an extreme position. To portray the world as a place of Sisyphean torture because it does not guarantee human beings invulnerability to injury and exemption from death is to assign fantastical importance to human beings. That our desires should be supremely important to us and that they should have a modest effect on what we seek from life is natural and reasonable, but that they should be thought to bind the universe borders on megalomania.

The same extremism shows itself in Camus's theory of truth. Human beings desire with all their being to know everything. We want to be certain, to see the point of things with perfect lucidity. This is the "nostalgia" Camus often speaks of.[17] What is our actual competence? We are able to know very little—just three items, actually. First, by the direct testimony of our senses we are sure that there are objects before us: there is a world. What the world is we are most unsure. Even science in the end proves to be a tissue of probabilities and cognitive constructs. "Poetry," Camus calls it.[18] Second, we know we exist and that we feel and think such and such. The human "heart" is to this extent open to itself. With an intuitive directness we grasp the existence of ourselves and the flux of feelings and thoughts that compose our conscious life.[19] Third, we know that our situation is absurd.[20] These three are all the truth we have, and honesty demands that we preserve them and live by them. What the absurdist demands of himself "is to live *solely* with what he knows, to accommodate himself to what is, and to bring in nothing that is not certain. . . . He wants to find out if it is possible to live without appeal."[21]

Beyond this tiny core of lucidity the rest of the world rises before us as "absurd walls." Everywhere we look it is the same: other human beings, our own motives and behavior, our daily routine, physical objects, time, death—all things—are dense, strange, and threatening, a "horde of irrationals."

Is Camus saying that familiar objects and processes are totally unintelligible, that science is a mistake, that common sense is madness? Not at all. He acknowledges that there is considerable practical and probable information available. Camus is no nihilist. The problem is that what we know is very fragmentary, and to a human being this is intolerable. We wish to know with certainty

33

absolutely all that can be known. Relative knowledge is not enough; probability is beneath our dignity; mere practical wisdom is unworthy of us. Above all, the problem is spiritual. We wish to comprehend, to understand the purpose of all things and to participate in its realization. Clearly, nothing will meet Camus's ideal except that humanity itself should be God. "Understanding the world for a man is reducing it to the human," he says.[22] Only if we could dominate all reality and assimilate it into ourselves could we overcome its hostility and redeem its beauties.

4. THE FLAW IN ABSURDISM

On the positive side, we must acknowledge that Camus faces up to the destructive component of existence. He recognizes that there is destructivity as well as creativity at the heart of existence, and he does not pretend otherwise. Moreover, Camus does provide an answer of sorts to the problem of abandonment. Human beings, like Rieux and Tarrou, who rebel against sickness and death and fight those evils in the name of Life do achieve meaningful interchange with the ultimate dimensions of the world. They have Life as their ally and Death as their enemy, and they are significantly engaged. By placing themselves on the side of Life, they overcome isolation.

Nevertheless, it seems to me that Camus has not found the best way to deal with the destructive elements we all face. He accepts the fact that we suffer and die, but he does not accept the propriety of this predicament. As we see in the characters of Rieux and Tarrou, he opposes not only the death-dealing forces but the system which inflicts them upon us. Essentially, Camus deals with destructivity through combat with a part of existence itself. Camus's rebels, for all their honesty and courage, are engaged in futile warfare with parts of what is natural and proper in the human condition. As I shall argue shortly, there is a better way.

We must conclude, I think, that Camus's basic problem resides in his inordinate idea of human greatness. Camus demands too much of life. If we expect to understand perfectly the purpose of all things and to be exempt from tragedy and death, then of course we will be basically frustrated and finally unhappy in this world. On such terms, only an omnipotent, omniscient being *could* be happy. And this is precisely the point: underneath it all, Camus is distressed because humanity is not God. In the final analysis, Camus's noble humanism is one more instance of humanity's perennial desire to deify itself. It interprets the widespread mood of abandonment as an opportunity for human beings to discover their own spiritual infinity, and it assumes that this expansion of the human spirit is the way, ideally, to cope with abandonment. However, Camus knows too well the frailties of the human spirit to think that the deification of the species—much less of any individual—could be carried through in fact. Humanity should, but never can, be God. As the master Hegel taught a century earlier and Camus's colleague Sartre repeats today, human beings are an "unhappy consciousness"—aware simultaneously of their potential infinity and of their incurable actual finitude. To twentieth-century stoicism, however, Camus adds one fillip which in my opinion makes it superior to Hegel's earlier and Sartre's later versions. He sees Sisyphus as happy—not ecstatic at realizing his own infinite potential, not blissful at establishing life-giving communication and peace with the deepest level of reality—but proud that in accepting the joys and frustrations of his individual life, he is doing all that a truthful person possibly can.

One should not be beguiled by the excellence of Camus's novels and the nobility of his humanistic convictions. His absurdism is antithetical to the principles of theistic belief. Camus accepts the *fact* but not the *propriety* of humanity's status as creature, and without this, genuine belief is impossible. Moreover, Camus insists that the honest and courageous person will "accept death as the only reality and live without hope,"[23] which is impossible for the Christian theist, who is sustained by the gospel proclamation that there is indeed hope, joy, and eternal life for all who believe in Jesus Christ.

Thus, the question John Loose asks in his useful article on Camus and the Christian, "Is it possible for a Christian to be an 'absurd man' as Camus describes that term?" can only be answered, contrary to Loose's judgment, in the negative.[24] True, there are some points of agreement. As Loose correctly observes, like the absurd man the Christian has to "realize that human reason has limits, and to admit that his knowledge has uncertainties."[25] Also, the absurd man can help Christians become aware of flaws in their own thinking and behavior—unchristian aspects of their Christianity. He can teach Christians that they should commit themselves far more than they have ever done before to "unceasing struggle and revolt, for creative freedom . . . in this life"; and he can teach Christians to discard that mistaken side of their concept of God which "demands [slavish] submission and obedience."[26]

Beyond this, however, the commonality ends. Camus's "living without appeal" is essentially what Kierkegaard would term "masculine despair." Camus's absurd man is conscious of having an affinity for eternity, but he resolves to place no one above himself. He is a creature who will not accept being a creature.

5. A CHRISTIAN RESPONSE TO ABSURDITY

Let us return to *The Plague* and imagine a fourth death, not this time of a child, a spiteful small-minded priest, or an atheist saint, but of a mature Christian. Let us call him Monsieur Courage, symbolizing a quality which he should exhibit in the face of the plague, whether it be a peaceful passing or the torture of the damned. Visualize how he responds to the agonies of Oran—how he views the deaths of others, how he understands his own illness, how he dies.

The first point to note is that M. Courage brings his own set of expectations to the experience. He assumes that the epidemic is a natural part of the created order. Bubonic plague is not a symbol of the demonic depths of existence, nor is it a direct manifestation of divine displeasure. Paneloux errs in preaching that God sends the plague to punish the people for their lack of spiritual ardor. No doubt the plague could function in some such way. It could serve to make the people conscious of their failings and bring them to penitence; and since God created the natural order, one could say that in this very general sense the plague is *intended* by God to be a punishment and a stimulus to reform human failings. However, this is all the truth I can see in the traditional Christian argument that evil occurs as divine punishment. God does not, like an irate parent, direct specific acts of punishment against specific acts of wrongdoing. There is more of randomness, looseness, and generality in the world than this.

Bubonic plague is an illness which occurs when human beings are infected by a certain bacillus carried by the fleas of rodents. It has no direct correlation with the moral or spiritual merit of its victims. It can be dealt with medically and prevented if certain precautions are taken. It can be cured or palliated if proper prophylactic measures are

37

applied. Plague is just an unfortunate possibility included in the world which God has created. It is a consequence of the incompatibility between two of God's creatures—plague bacilli and human beings. Plague is one of the imperfections in a mostly good and always magnificent world. It is not a manifestation of malevolence in nature, nor is it a symbol of the essential ill disposition of the creator. Plague reveals the vulnerability of all things and reminds us that all living beings in their season die.

It is with some such convictions that M. Courage approaches the appalling events of the plague in Oran, and because of these convictions he behaves in distinctive ways. There is an equanimity in his reaction to the first deaths. It is not like Tarrou's reaction, based in curiosity and a desire to comprehend everything. M. Courage's essential passion is a deep confidence in the basic goodness of things. He does not panic, and he does not recoil from contact with others. What the plague teaches the others about the importance of intrahuman solidarity, he already knows. What it teaches the thoughtless ones about the value of human life, he already knows. All persons share a common destiny, and sooner or later all die. However, combined with this sad awareness is a more basic joy. Life is prior to death. Life is granted to each person by one who is Life itself, and it is ours for a brief period to be used and enjoyed. No matter how brief one's time may be, it is a supreme value. Here M. Courage differs completely from M. Tarrou. What counts first is not that we have a quantity of life, but that we exist at all. We exist *now* although we might have perished yesterday or ten years ago. We shall probably exist *tomorrow*. Every moment is a supreme and complete value, for it is a triumph over nonexistence, an unearned, uncertain, and gratefully received value.

Thus, M. Courage views the deaths around him as

incapable of destroying the worth and meaning of human existence. The bewilderment, fear, panic, and suspicion which seize the general citizenry will pass over him. This does not mean that he does not have negative feelings. What is precious one wishes to keep as long as possible, and when it is gone one feels an emptiness. M. Courage may weep, for his heart is not less sensitive than those of others. Moreover, like M. Tarrou, he seeks to be alert, to see clearly what is happening and how it involves him. However, his motivation is that what is happening is intrinsically important and invites his participation, not that it is meaningless until he endows it with meaning.

M. Courage works to counter the plague as energetically as any M. Tarrou or Dr. Rieux. Rieux does not spend more energy or take more risks to treat the ill; Tarrou does not labor more carefully to sanitize the clinics and hospitals. M. Courage uses all his skills, and no one is more hopeful that the epidemic will be broken. Moreover, he is concerned about long-range prevention, and he raises questions about whether proper measures of cleanliness and inoculation are being followed. Although he grants that human beings must die, he does not agree that just these deaths are inevitable. He works to maximize the quality of life and to provide the greatest longevity consistent with quality. He says, as passionately as Dr. Rieux, that he refuses to love a system which puts little children, or indeed anyone, to torture. He does not view the magistrate's child's last moments as torture, however, but as the tragic price some persons must pay for the opportunity of existing on this earth. Unlike Rieux, Courage does not assume that God could prevent the plague.

This is our imagined Christian in his relation to the deaths of others. He has been sketched as positively as possible; but he has not yet been put to the full test. How will he face his own death? "Then Satan answered the Lord, 'Does Job fear God for nought? Hast thou not put a hedge about him and his house? . . . But put forth thy hand now, and touch his bone and flesh, and he will curse thee to thy face.'" (Job 1:9-10a–2:5) It is one thing to respond to the tragedies of others and another to respond to one's own. What does M. Courage do when the plague poisons his own flesh and bone? First, he does not lapse into the mute resignation we see in Father Paneloux. Fatalism has no place in a Christian life. Even if one believes that in a sense the plague and the fact that one has contracted plague are God's will, one must not submit to this will as if it were a dire inevitability. It may be built into the structure of the human situation (and thus foreordained in a general way) that human beings, under certain conditions, will contract certain diseases. It may even be foreordained that given certain actual disease-generating conditions, specific persons exposed to those conditions will contract this disease. Even so, when the disease comes, it is not caused by fate; it is not just an imposed condition to which we must submit. Father Paneloux is wrong to lie motionless upon his bed, wrong to make himself plastic to powerful force. , wrong to say uncritically that we should love what we cannot understand. Everything depends on the sense in which the plague is in accord with God's will. Only something willed for humanity's benefit or for the benefit of the entire creation should be loved, and I do not think that this can be said about the plague. Although plague is a part of God's creation and thus a consequence of God's will, it is not, I think, something God willingly decrees for our benefit. It is, rather, an unavoidable accompaniment of the system; we must bear it, but we need not love it. Paneloux invites us to mystification in saying we should love what we cannot understand. There are many things humanity cannot understand, and we are under no obligation to love all of them. Not every event which seems unintelligible to our human, all too human, intelligence is God's direct intention. The world contains not only mystery (that is, more than humanly intelligible, divinely wrought occurrences), but outright irrationality; and part of the human task is to try to distinguish them. Since the world is not God and contains its share of imperfections and obscurity, we are sometimes entitled to oppose, even hate, parts of it. Needless suffering and death are examples. I should say that it is God's will that we should struggle against them, that we should fight to preserve life. This holds true even though by God's will we are mortal. Although we must die sometime, we cannot know until we have drunk deeply of an experience that this is our time. Whenever it is to our benefit, we are called to act in concert with God against the negative features of the order which God has created. It is possible that we are called to resist this death now, although we are, as mortals, not to resist all death. If Paneloux says amen to human mortality, he speaks Christianly, but if he says amen to whatever happens, he deifies it and delivers himself into the hands of fate.

Thus, M. Courage would turn away from the deathbed of Father Paneloux, disgusted. He wants more spirit, a more forceful affirmation of life; he wants practical evidence of a belief that God is in the world overcoming death to the fullest extent that is possible and beneficial for mortal beings. He resolves to meet his own death, when it comes, with striving.

Imagine, then, that the plague at last reaches M. Courage. He feels the fever and the painful lumps beneath his arms; he experiences in his own flesh the debilities he has been observing in others. Now he begins his own fight. Like Tarrou, he stands on the side of life. Each surge

41

toward death he meets with an affirmation of life; to every negative he counterposes a positive. M. Courage will hold to life as long as strength allows and good sense dictates. He will do so with God's help, that is, in the conviction that the Creator is present and actively involved in his struggle. He will believe that his holding on to life is consonant with God's will, and he will visualize physical life as augmented and supported by an undercurrent of divine Life. The struggle is better understood as *for* life than *against* death. It is a partnership, a sharing, an agreement between one tiny, transient being and Life itself.

At the same time, M. Courage's attachment to life, that is, to staying alive, is not an absolute. Aware of his essential mortality, he does not insist that life not be taken away from him. He is prepared to yield. He is convinced that merely being alive in this mind-body is not an ultimate state. For the creature, dying is an essential ingredient in living, and it is as important to die well as to live well. Dying well is not simply refusing to the end to go gently into that dark night. M. Courage believes that the moment will arrive when it is God's intention for him to surrender, and he has been forewarned that he will not know his own hour. It is Courage's responsibility, as long as he is able, to decide whether this is indeed his hour.

M. Courage tries to preserve his life, then, but differently than Tarrou. He is free of desperation, free of the hatred which confrontation with an enemy inevitably engenders, free of pessimism, and free of the final aura of defeat. When he is finally still, the smile which rests on his lips expresses the satisfaction of one who loves life first but accepts death when it comes, as his due. He is one who reveres God above all and values human life neither more nor less than it warrants. If anyone deserves to be considered a saint, he does.

CHAPTER 2

BETRAYAL

1. THE SUPREME ABSURDITY

We have been considering the suffering which all human beings, as human beings, experience. Now we turn to the suffering which certain groups inflict on other groups—at the behest or connivance, some would say, of God himself. In this chapter we consider the Holocaust; in following chapters, racism and sexism.

When we permit ourselves to think openly about the Nazi assault upon Jewry, we see concretely what is meant by absurdity. Here was institutionalized irrationality, organized destructivity, programmed nihilism—the ultimate in the sadistic use of human efficiency. Even those who do not feel the mood of abandonment must be deeply troubled by the Holocaust—if for one instant they allow themselves to face it. How can the Holocaust possibly be reconciled with the traditional belief that every human being is precious in God's eyes and that Jews are especially beloved? How can destruction of such diabolic magnitude occur in a world ordered by a God of love and justice?

It is presumptuous of me to venture judgments about a tragedy which I did not personally experience, and it is precarious to interpret theologically the perceptions of a religion which is not my own; yet I do not see how I can plausibly advocate belief in the one God of all humankind unless I do so. I can only hope that the limitations of my theological perspective will not too much distort what I see, and I must ask forbearance where my observations are unjust or insensitive. Moreover, it may be said that Christian theologians cannot afford not to deal with the Holocaust. As Alice Eckardt points out, the Holocaust is not just a Jewish problem, it is a Christian problem;[1] and as Paul J. Kirsch says, "considering the involvement of Christians in the existence of antisemitism," Christians simply must join with Jews in "working on the problem of understanding the holocaust." We may not "act as if nothing had happened."[2] The future of Christendom waits upon our judgments about many Holocaust-related issues. Why did Christian beliefs supply the Nazis with ideological justifications, and why did Christians take part, actively or tacitly, in the persecutions? Why have Christians been silent for so long, and why are they even today not eager to discuss the Holocaust? However difficult it may be, it is better to speak than to remain silent. Perhaps Emil Fackenheim is right when he says that many contemporary Christians have experienced the death of God because they have not faced their own complicity in the Holocaust.[3]

What we shall do, therefore, is try to comprehend how the Holocaust could have occurred if, as the Bible teaches, the world is ruled by a God of wisdom, justice, and power who loves all humanity and cares for Jews as its special people. We shall examine the conclusions of several contemporary Jewish theologians who believe that because of the Holocaust it is virtually impossible to believe any longer in the God of history. We shall give special attention to the reflections of Emil Fackenheim, who is acutely sensitive to both sides of the question and labors mightily to find a sane path between outright denial of God and straight traditional acceptance.

2. FAITH AFTER AUSCHWITZ

The Holocaust, of course, has had a profoundly threatening effect on the faith of Jews. It cast millions of persons into despair and put their faith under strains which are scarcely bearable. It confirmed the unbelief of some who already disbelieved and precipitated decisions of unbelief in others. In one noteworthy case it led to the sad conclusion that the God of history is dead. Rabbi Richard Rubenstein, to the consternation of many of his colleagues, argued that if history is the "unfolding of the Divine drama of mankind's salvation . . . some very unpleasant conclusions necessarily follow. . . . It was God's will that Hitler had exterminated the Jews." If God is "the ultimate actor in the historical drama, no other theological interpretation of the death of six million Jews is tenable."[4] Nevertheless, it is a fact that the Holocaust did not destroy the faith of the vast majority of Jews. They continued to believe in God whether or not they could find good reasons for doing so.

Emil Fackenheim is one who continues to believe. From his own experience with nazism, he understands the agony of his fellow religionists. He shares their despair and feels the same pressure of the evidence leading toward denial. He agrees with Rubenstein that the absurdity of Auschwitz seems to belie the presence of the God of history. Nevertheless, he refuses to give up either God or the belief in Jewish chosenness.

What are Fackenheim's reasons? Working within what he calls the "Midrashic framework," he appeals to tradition for guidance. What have the rabbis said before about similar tragedies? What are sensitive Jews who know their tradition now saying to account for Auschwitz?

Fackenheim reviews the traditional midrashic doctrines which might be thought to explain Auschwitz, and he rejects them all. The familiar "for our sins we are punished" principle he dismisses because "however we twist and turn this doctrine in response to Auschwitz, it becomes a religious absurdity and even a sacrilege."[5] Those Midrashim which would explain Auschwitz as martyrdom are also unsuitable. Although some Jews died with a courage which glorified God, most were simply herded to their deaths like cattle.[6] The "Midrashim of protest" cannot explain Auschwitz either, because no amount of protest can restore the slain children or deepen the survivors' sense of God's presence. In deference to those who perished, Jews today must "refuse comfort."[7] The "Midrashim of powerlessness" Fackenheim sets aside because in pagan Europe there was no fear of God and thus no possibility of anyone's being brought to God by Jewish suffering. Powerlessness only incites sadism.[8] Finally, the "Midrashim of exile" prove unsatisfactory. The Holocaust was no mere temporary separation from God. There will be no return to Zion for the Six Million. The time for the Messiah to come was *then;* a "Messiah who is able to come but who at Auschwitz did not come, has become an impossibility."[9]

Thus, no matter how we maneuver theologically, the conclusion is inescapable: the Holocaust cannot be explained or justified. It stands in all its absurdity, darkening the past and casting an ominous shadow over the future of all humanity. Up to this point, Fackenheim is in essential agreement with Rubenstein; logically, Auschwitz implies that God does not exist. However, Fackenheim does not draw that conclusion. On the contrary, he maintains that Jews should refuse to deny God, that, indeed, they are forbidden to do so. How does Fackenheim reach this position? How does he know Jews must not turn away in disbelief?

The basic evidence is the satanic nature of nazism. The

Jew was "singled out by a demonic power which sought his death absolutely, i.e., as an end in itself."[10] No Jew—not even the most convinced secularist—can escape this much of the supernatural. Jews know "that the devil, if not God, is alive." Further, all should recognize that this absolute negation must be countered with an absolute affirmation. Someone must will Jewish *life* as totally as the demons of nazism willed Jewish *death*.[11] However, no mere human being is capable of an absolute action. Only God is absolutely good and able to ground an absolute defense of Jewish life. "Jewish opposition to the demons of Auschwitz cannot be understood in terms of humanly created ideals . . . but only as an imposed commandment . . . an imperative as truly given—as the Voice of Sinai."[12]

In this way the Jews begin to hear the "commanding Voice of Auschwitz," which instructs them: (1) to remember and to tell the story of the Holocaust, (2) to survive as Jews, (3) to fight for a humane world, (4) to continue to wrestle with God.[13] There could be no greater mistake, no deeper tragedy after Auschwitz, than to give up God and thus do for Hitler what he could not do for himself—destroy Judaism. "Jews are forbidden to hand Hitler posthumous victories. . . . They are forbidden to despair of the God of Israel, lest Judaism perish."[14]

What is this Voice of Auschwitz? Is Fackenheim saying that in the Holocaust the Jew somehow *encounters* God and hears him *decree* that Judaism must not perish? Is the Commanding Voice God himself? This may be what Fackenheim intends to convey, and I suspect that it is what he would *like* to say. However, it is not at all clear that he is prepared to go this far.[15] A second look at the four commands from Auschwitz will reveal a definite reservation about the nature of the Voice. Fackenheim does not actually say that it is God who speaks; he does not announce "Thus saith the Lord." The Voice could be a personification of the violated rights of the persons who perished; it could be the projection of the outrage and protest of the survivors; it could be a verbalization of contemporary Jews' desire to survive. Fackenheim's hesitation on this point prompts philosopher Michael Wyschogrod to comment that Fackenheim's analysis of Auschwitz yields "a kind of negative, natural theology with the survival of the people, rather than the existence of God, as the conclusion." [16]

Fackenheim's indecision about whether to identify the Voice as God is seen explicitly in his unwillingness to agree with Elie Wiesel that the Holocaust is comparable with Sinai in revelatory significance. Fackenheim shrinks from "this daring comparison." It cannot be said that God reveals himself in such diabolism. At the same time, however, Fackenheim shrinks "even more" from the opposite position of "not listening" to the Voice and seeking a "false refuge in endless agnosticism"; "in faithfulness to Judaism we must refuse to disconnect God from the Holocaust." [17]

Thus, Jews are caught in an agonizingly ambiguous position. Because of the Holocaust they cannot confidently affirm God; yet, again because of the Holocaust they are forbidden to deny God. They hold tenaciously to their traditional belief, trusting against all contrary evidence that it is true. They continue, as Fackenheim puts it, to "wrestle with God." [18] This is why Fackenheim prefers novelist Elie Wiesel's contemporary midrash as a clue to the Holocaust. Wiesel writes of the "slightly mad" Jew who one night during the worst years of the Nazi persecution burst in upon a synagogue service and warned the worshipers not to pray so loudly because God might hear them and realize that there were some Jews left alive. This sad paradox expresses the plight of the post-Auschwitz Jew. Even as he prays he fears God will hear and send him to his death.

Unlike Nietzsche's madman, who boldly announces in the marketplace that God is dead, the Jew wavers: should he reaffirm his ancient faith, or should he declare God dead? In the memory of Auschwitz, neither seems appropriate; therefore, he does what he can—he prays, but softly, lest he be heard.

3. MIDRASHIC PARADOX

Actually, Fackenheim points out, the conflict which the Holocaust poses for faith is nothing new, in principle, to those who reason within a midrashic framework. Midrashic questioning accepts the unresolvable contradictoriness of the "root experiences of Judaism." What human being can understand how the just and loving Lord of all humanity could choose to deliver Israel from slavery by drowning his other children, the Egyptians?[19] What human mind can comprehend a God who is at once transcendent *and* immanent, eternal *and* linked with time, unchanging *and* involved in historical process?[20] At its best, human understanding of such a God must be fragmentary and contradictory. Thus, those who approach God in the spirit of the Midrash will reflect on "the contradictions in the root experiences" of Judaism, knowing *a priori* that they "cannot resolve [them] . . . but only express them . . . in story, parable, and metaphor."[21] Jews know that they can neither entirely comprehend their encounters with God nor deny and alter them without denying God and, therefore, themselves. In this we see what Fackenheim calls "the logic of midrashic stubbornness."[22] "The Midrash holds fast to the *truth* of these contradictory affirmations even as it expresses their contradictoriness. . . . The rabbinic thinker both *reflects upon* his relation to God and yet *stands directly before* Him, and his theology is consciously and

49

stubbornly fragmentary."[23] Even from the ashes of the Holocaust the rabbinic theologian will not deny God.

This methodology clearly has important—and I think questionable—consequences for Fackenheim's treatment of the Holocaust. It is basically what justifies his refusal to give up God without accounting for the Holocaust. Since God's actions always largely escape human understanding, anyone who believes in God *must* accept some irrationality. The question is whether they can accept total irrationality. The Holocaust becomes the supreme test of faith. Will this paramount irrationality destroy faith, or can Jews overcome it as they have every other lesser irrationality? It is clear why Fackenheim affirms the appropriateness of Wiesel's midrash about the half-mad Jew who prays, but too softly for God to hear.

4. ACCOUNTING FOR THE HOLOCAUST

Let us now appraise Fackenheim's argument. Does he offer reasons which warrant our continuing to believe in the God of providential power? Can I find here help for my own project of reconciling belief in God with the occurrence of radical evil?

Many will think Fackenheim's ambivalent commitment to belief less plausible than Rubenstein's forthright denial of God. There is something clean and decisive about the latter's declaration: "I have elected to accept what Camus has rightly called the courage of the absurd, the courage to live in a meaningless, purposeless Cosmos rather than believe in a God who inflicts Auschwitz on his people."[24] I agree with this determination to get at the reasons underlying the Holocaust and the refusal to hold to traditional answers just because they are venerable. Nevertheless, I find Rubenstein's delineation of the alternatives too narrow. We are not restricted to believing that either God does not exist or that "at Auschwitz my people stood under the most fearsome curse that God ever inflicted."[25] We can rethink the meaning of divine power and human freedom and seek to redefine the traditional understanding of the God-world relation. I prefer to stand with Fackenheim in refusing to give up believing in the God of history. I respect and admire his perseverance in faith in spite of the Holocaust, and I agree with his warnings about the limits of human speculation. Statements about God are indeed about the Unique One, the Creator who is beyond time yet acts in time, and who is simultaneously eternal and involved in history. Theological statements are indeed made by human beings, creatures of time, who think from within the uncompleted flow of history. Given the human, all too human, perspective of the theologian, it is not surprising that theology should be constitutionally subject to inconsistency and fragmentariness.

Nevertheless, it seems to me that at certain crucial points Fackenheim is overly cautious. After all his deliberations on the Midrashim concerning suffering, he still cannot suggest any even partially plausible theological reason why Auschwitz occurred. He recoils from this. Psychologically, it is completely understandable. To claim to be able to rationalize this utter horror seems blasphemous. Better to let it stand in all its physical and moral repulsiveness. As a result, however, Fackenheim flees too quickly to midrashic stubbornness and settles too easily for too much fragmentariness and contradictoriness. He takes refuge in the midrash of the half-mad Jew when he should be moving boldly in a renewed effort to understand.

I should say that no case for belief in God in the post-Auschwitz time can be very convincing which does not dare to try to say *why* God willed Auschwitz. This no doubt will strike many as presumptuous and offensive, but it cannot be avoided. We do not have the logical right to believe in God until we come to terms with the horrifying problem of God's complicity in evil, until we find some reason for the staggering truth which belief in God entails—that in some sense God wills the death of the Six Million.

5. GOD'S POWER AT AUSCHWITZ

Very little can be done to account for the Holocaust, however, until we reject several traditional assumptions. First, we must reject the notion, which we have just seen in Fackenheim, that God's deeds in history are so clothed in paradox that we cannot understand our root experiences as God's people. If God is Truth, then whatever happens in God's world *must* have an explanation accessible to some degree to every rational creature. Even the Holocaust must be intelligible. Neither its admitted uniqueness nor its unparalleled savagery can entirely block our understanding. Although the Holocaust is in some ways unique, it is not entirely unlike what happened to Jews in earlier tragedies and to what has happened to other peoples.[26] It is best understood, in Michael Wyschogrod's words, as "a first among equals."[27]

I am not claiming that human beings are able to understand the Holocaust totally; I mean simply that a sufficiently informed analysis of its spiritual and social dynamics can uncover what breakdown in human decency and good sense led to it; and I mean that human beings can form a plausible notion of why God willed it.

Second, we must reject the assumption that God possesses *unqualified* power. This notion has intolerable implications. If God can do whatever it wishes, then it could have prevented Auschwitz. Since it did not, it must have wished for Auschwitz to happen; and if that is so, Auschwitz must be good and God must enjoy it. But if God enjoys Auschwitz, the human value system is totally subverted. Cruelty is kindness, agony is pleasure, injustice is justice. Humanity is plunged into moral madness.

If we could clear our heads of the assumption that God must possess absolute and unqualified power, Rubenstein would not have to deny God (nor subject us to his monstrous "Cannibal Mother" substitute),[28] Fackenheim would not have to take refuge in the mad Jew's prayer, and *no one* would have to accept the absurd proposition that God could and would have prevented the Holocaust but did not. If there are some things God cannot do, and if preventing the Holocaust is one of them, then God must not be charged with this atrocity against the Jewish people. Not God, but those who defied God's will are culpable.

No doubt this will seem blasphemous to many who wish to preserve what is called the sovereignty of God. Is God only one of many agents determining the flow of history? Is God merely somewhat more powerful than its creatures? As Tillich would say, is God merely *a* being alongside other beings? Such a view is not theism but atheism.

The point of this protest is plain enough. To some, limited power seems an imperfection—indeed it seems one of the generic imperfections which distinguish all creatures from the Creator—and if we admit it into God, we compromise God's worship-worthiness. However, I deny that holding to the traditional idea of omnipotence is the way to preserve God's worthiness. Actually, it does the opposite. A God who exercises total control over absolutely everything that happens and exercises its will regardless of the inclinations of those affected is not supreme goodness but sheer power—awesome but not deserving of worship. A God deserving of worship shares power with its creatures, allowing them, as far as possible, to make their own decisions, teaching them to decide wisely, controlling them by helping them control themselves. *Perfect* power nourishes the power in others, thus bringing new and greater power into being. Through its creatures' deeds, it calls into being absolutely new, voluntary motions. It gives existence to independent, living images of itself.

Thus, divine perfection *implies* limitation. Being perfectly powerful, God allows rational creatures room to think and choose for themselves. God makes them able to be wrong as well as right, foolish as well as wise; God arranges the world so that creatures can initiate and carry through projects both creative and destructive. God exercises "adequate" power, as Charles Hartshorne says; that is, God does for the world everything which can "be done and need be done by one universal or cosmic agent" and leaves to "local agents" the power and right to do as much as they can for themselves.[29]

What we have just said about limits in God suggests that we should look again at the Midrashim of powerlessness. As we saw earlier, Fackenheim rejects this position because to the nations of the modern world, who do not believe in God, powerlessness is an invitation to exploitation. Powerlessness means further holocausts. We must determine whether this is true, for if it is, my case for divine powerlessness should be dropped. Let us note something that Fackenheim says about one of Elie Wiesel's stories in the novel *Night*. He says, deprecatingly, that whereas in the traditional Midrashim "God is only 'as it were' powerless, in *Night*, Wiesel sees Him in the face of a child hanging on the gallows."[30] That is, Wiesel dares to envision the possibility that God, like those children who died in the camps, *cannot* defend himself and his people against the Nazi murderers.

This "as it were" says a great deal about Fackenheim's

earlier discussion of powerlessness. It means that he was not thinking of God as *really* powerless. God *withholds* his power and goes along with his people into exile, trying in this *simulation* of defenselessness to move the consciences of the errant nations and bring them to righteousness. It means that God *voluntarily* submits himself and his chosen children to the slaughter of the Holocaust. No wonder Fackenheim recoils. The thought that God and the Jewish people would knowingly yield to sadists and murderers is surely too terrible to consider seriously. This is the practical equivalent of suicide.

What shall we say to this? First, let us observe that, given this sense of powerlessness, Fackenheim does not really grapple with full divine powerlessness, wherein God *literally* cannot prevent the Holocaust. Full powerlessness cannot be summarily dismissed as suicidal or as denying Jews the right to defend themselves, for it implies only that God cannot prevent the Holocaust. Human beings, on the other hand, are free—indeed, obligated—to do what they can to protect their rights. Further, and more importantly, Fackenheim rejects full divine powerlessness for the reason expressed in the following passage:

> To stake all on divine powerlessness today, therefore, would be to take it both radically and literally. God suffers literal and radical powerlessness, i.e., actual death; and any resurrected divine power will be manifest, not so much within history as beyond it. A Jew, in short, would have to become a Christian. But . . . never in the two thousand years of Jewish-Christian confrontation has it been less possible for a Jew to abandon either his Jewishness or his Judaism and embrace Christianity.[31]

In short, Fackenheim draws back from the concept of real divine powerlessness because he believes that it requires Jews to become Christians and to give up all hope for deliverance from injustice in this life.

55

I see no reason to think that these two ruinous consequences must follow from divine powerlessness of the sort favored here. In the first place, Jews need not become Christians to believe that God is limited in power. The idea that God can be defied, impeded, and entangled in the errors and wickedness of the world is not exclusively Christian. It is based on the central biblical theme of the covenant and of God's long-suffering effort to win and keep the love of its people. Again and again in the biblical narrative God's will for humankind is negated; and each time God sends someone through whom the alienation is overcome: Noah, Abraham, Moses, the Judges, the Prophets, Saul, David, Solomon. Surely this view of a God who can be temporarily thwarted by human beings is at least as Jewish as Christian. And can it not be applied to the Holocaust? Do I not hear Jewish philosopher Hans Jonas speaking about the Holocaust with essentially this image of a God who from the beginning of creation suffers with its creatures in an effort to bring them to a high level of consciousness and morality?[32]

Fackenheim's other reason for opposing the concept of a powerless God—that it invites further holocausts—seems to me equally unconvincing. In the first place, the doctrine says only that God is unable to do *certain* things, not that it is totally helpless. Admittedly, God cannot intervene and stop the Holocaust the way police rush in to stop a crime, but this does not mean that God did not strive to prevent it and might not have succeeded. Nor does it imply that God lacks the power to prevent future holocausts. If enough human beings respond to the inducements of God, God will overcome our destructiveness. What God cannot do is override our free determinations by some magical intervention. Never again will God send the Great Flood to expunge human wickedness; or, more accurately, never again may we think that this is the way God works; never again may we believe that such simple deliverance is possible.

Nevertheless, there is power in this powerlessness. God is there, working on the destructive human agencies, quietly seeking to turn them around. Moreover, even at Auschwitz God apparently had some success. God reached those of the victims who endured their suffering with dignity and courage, those friends who consoled or sheltered the potential victims, those intrepid rebels, Jews and non-Jews, who had the strength to resist openly; God even touched, however slightly, those equivocal and silent ones who at least felt troubled in conscience by what they knew or suspected was going on. In more obvious ways, God was active in the liberating armies and agencies of relief which cooperated to overthrow the Nazi madness.

It is true that this power was totally insufficient for the millions who perished. Nevertheless, it is all that was possible if God was to respect human beings as moral agents and creators of value. As Jewish theologian Eliezer Berkovits observes, "God cannot as a rule intervene whenever man's use of freedom displeases him." To do so would abolish good and evil and man as well. The real question is not "Why is there undeserved suffering? But why is there man?"[33] As long as we believe in the inherent value of human beings and credit them with the power to create value, we know the answer to that question. Whoever says that Auschwitz absolutely should not have occurred and that God should, at all costs, have prevented it, says that human beings should not exist.

6. EVIL AND GOD'S WILL

The Holocaust occurred because God wills radical evil as a possibility in this world and because human beings, contrary to God's primary intention, willed to translate that perverse possibility into actuality. The Holocaust occurred because God, willing it as a possibility and human freedom as an actuality, *had* to concur in its actualization. Yielding to humanity's insistence on this outbreak of destruction, God willed Auschwitz as a secondary intention.

Once more, it is the inevitability of this divine move which needs to be stressed. Given genuine human self-determination, it is inevitable that God be involved in the evils which flaw the world, and it is inevitable that the world be flawed. The first is so because God makes us free, knowing that we will sin. The second is so because only God can be absolute perfection. The world is other than absolute perfection and therefore is necessarily imperfect in some way. As imperfect, it is vulnerable to evil. God is eternal, but the world begins and ends; God is constant in goodness, but the world errs, loses its way, chooses unwisely. Only this way can the world be decisively other than God.

Does this mean that the world *is* evil? Do we say that whatever is not God is evil? On the contrary, it means that the world is good, that it possesses different kinds and degrees of good but in finite form, which is the only form open to the world if it is to be other than God. "Good" is used here in a broad sense, as referring to degrees of fullness of being. The richer and more complete a being is, the greater its degree of good. This obviously is not primarily a moral notion of good, but an ontological one. Being is good; and God, as perfect being, is perfect good. The world and its numberless beings are relative goods. The appropriate evaluation here is more esthetic than moral. It is similar to when God pauses from the labor of creation and looks upon all that it has made and sees that it is "very good." God does not speak of moral goodness, for in that pristine moment, all is innocence. God speaks of the worth of existence and expresses joy and satisfaction that the world exists and that it contains just these beings.

The world as finite in its goodness is not evil but imperfect, and it is this not because it lacks something which it ought to have, but simply because it is not perfection as such, not that goodness than which a greater goodness cannot be conceived. The term "evil" is reserved for those features of the world which develop out of the world's intrinsic imperfections. The world is not evil, but it is vulnerable to evil, and sooner or later it will be marred by it. Evil, then, is the loss of some appropriate value already possessed, or the failure to acquire some value needed or innocently desired.

Why is this world inevitably flawed by evil? Because it is derivative and temporal. In its totality and in all of its parts the world comes to be and passes away. No being lasts for long. Moreover, even while it lasts it is unstable. New qualities are acquired only through the breakdown and loss of old qualities. Growth comes only after decay, birth only after death; such is the pattern of the world. Moreover, beings seldom acquire all the goods they need and never achieve all they might. There is too much interference within the system, too much competition among beings in pursuit of the same value. Moreover, the world does not contain enough value to satisfy every desire and probably not enough to satisfy every need. There is no way that such a burgeoning, overlapping, densely populated, continuously changing, fragile world can avoid evil; and there is no way that its Creator, who is Lord of history, can avoid being involved in evil.

Nor is that all. Since God is Creator, it is not only involved in the evil of the world but *ultimately responsible* for it. It is God who is responsible for the fact that there is a world and for the fact that the world is just the world it is. God is even responsible indirectly for the evil choices of human beings—even for the butchers of Auschwitz—because in its omniscience it knows the likelihood of those evil choices. God creates, *knowing* they will, or probably will, occur, knowing that in order to create just this world it must become an accomplice in evil. I see no way the theist can escape this melancholy implication.

At the same time, there is no need to say that God wills the *evil* of the evil events. As Alasdair MacIntyre points out, there is an ambiguity in the sentence "Everything happens by the will of God," which can be eliminated if we say that "God wills that men should do what they will, even if it is not what God would wish them to do."[34] Thus there is a reservation in God's willing the world. God consents freely and fully to our right to do what we will, but resistingly to any evil we do. For the sake of creaturely creativity, God exposes the divine good to contradiction. There is tragedy at the heart of God's will to create.

This should not obscure the positive side of creation, however. God is compelled by nothing. It freely creates, knowing what is involved. God willingly allows the frustrations of its aims, assumes the ultimate responsibility for the evil that is done, opens itself to the suffering which comes with the world's suffering. This is the price God is prepared to pay and the measure of the high value God puts on the world. Only if God endures such negativity can there be the radical increment of being that the creation of this world brings. Existence, with all its negativities, is worth even the Holocaust.

I am agreeing with Berkovits when he says that God is obliged to create the possibility of evil in order to establish the possibility of good; however, I am going beyond that and saying that indirectly God also creates the *actuality* of evil. I think it is misleading to say, as Berkovits does, that "God renounces the use of his power" on human history.[35] It is not a matter of renunciation but of inability. God does not infallibly control human history—that is, it does not deal with human beings in the same way it deals with atoms and galaxies—because this cannot be done. Human beings are categorically different from atoms and galaxies. The very concept of a totally manipulated human being is a contradiction, a nonsensical concept, as incapable of actualization as a round square. If God wants this world, it must will the evil which its creatures enact.

We must decide whether we can agree with God that the value of this world is sufficient to justify the suffering. Some will think not; they will feel that the level of human creativity should be scaled down to limit the level of human destructiveness. This is an exceedingly difficult discrimination to make. Perhaps a less inventive but happier, more secure human existence would be preferable to what we have. The Holocaust may be the conclusive evidence for this. I did not experience the death camps and cannot say. However, because of the Holocaust I know that in the future any group, my own included, may suffer a similar fate, and I am prepared to say that in spite of this, it is best that human beings remain as they are, with no less potential for greatness and no less potential for degradation. I am prepared to say that, all things considered, it is fitting that this very world exist; if God had not created this world, it should have.

I do not think that this commits us to saying that Auschwitz is a good thing and that the world would be deficient without it; but it does imply that the world would be deficient without the *possibility* of Auschwitz, because it would not be a place where freedom carries the maximum of risk and persons bear the full consequences of their actions. Auschwitz is the cost God is willing to pay (and asks us to be willing to pay) for a world in which human beings are capable of participating significantly in the ongoing work of creation. Auschwitz is a price we need not have paid, but now that we have, we must not let it cause despair. Perhaps Ignaz Maybaum is correct that Auschwitz is *churban*, "a catastrophe which makes an end to an old era and creates a new era";[36] perhaps it is such a rare turning point in the history of God's redemption of the human race that henceforth a holocaust is unthinkable. The Holocaust speaks not only to Jews but to all human beings, and it tells of the radical evil which has been in the world as a possibility from the beginning and which threatens us all, at all times. Because of the Holocaust we know the depths to which humanity can fall.

Elie Wiesel's *Gates of the Forest* is an autobiographical novel about the plight of Hungarian Jews under the Nazis. Gregor, the chief character, is a young man whose family have been taken away, and who manages to survive only by living as a fugitive in the desolate countryside. Years after the end of the war, Gregor, who has lost his faith, asks a Hasidic rebbe how he can continue to believe in God after "what has happened to us." The rebbe replies: "How can you not believe in God after what has happened?" This does not satisfy Gregor, and he continues to argue passionately. Finally, the rebbe makes a concession, which I think is consonant with what I am arguing.

> "So be it!" he shouted. "He's guilty; do you think I don't know it? That I have no eyes to see, no ears to hear? That my heart doesn't revolt? That I have no desire to beat my head against the wall and shout like a madman, to give rein to my sorrow and disappointment? Yes, he is guilty. He has become the ally of evil, of death, of

murder, but the problem is still not solved. I ask you a question and dare you to answer: 'What is there left for us to do?'"[37]

If the argument of this chapter is sound, we can see our way clear to offering an answer to this question. We are called to understand that God has become the ally of evil, death, and murder so that we may have the miracle of creativity and may bear the divine image in our hearts; and we are called to use this miracle for good. There must never be another Holocaust.

CHAPTER 3

HATRED

We turn now to the second of the humanly inflicted forms of radical human suffering—racism. Racism is less spectacular, less apocalyptic than the Holocaust, but no less—and some would say more—devastating to the souls and bodies of its victims.[1]

Racism is a third dimension of absurdity. There is something crushingly irrational about a world in which one group of people are systematically denied access to normal opportunities for education and employment, are subjugated economically, humiliated socially, harassed, and on occasion murdered—for no other reason than the color of their skin. It is small wonder that black theologian James Cone—although strongly committed to a Christian outlook—invokes Camus's concept of absurdity to characterize the position of blacks in white society,[2] and that black philosopher William R. Jones asks whether God has a "demonic streak" and hates blacks.[3] Certainly on Christian premises racism is absurd. A just, omnicompetent, loving God would treat all of its children kindly and fairly and would not tolerate a situation in which one group is singled out for suffering which is "maldistributed, enormous, dehumanizing, and transgenerational."[4] Indeed, since God has created human beings as they are, it is difficult to understand how they could even *want* to exploit one another. Is God so inept a creator?

1. BLACK THEOCENTRIC THEISM

It is precisely this raw inconsistency between God's supposed benevolence and the mistreatment of blacks which inspires William R. Jones to pose his odd and shocking question, "Is God a white racist?" This query is not intended merely as an arresting book title, but as a way of calling attention to a neglected and provocative theological possibility. Jones is convinced that black theologians have not faced up to this possibility, have not admitted that hatred of blacks is not precluded by the concept of God which they have accepted from the Christian tradition. If God is sovereign over history, as this tradition holds, then what happens in history—including the oppression of blacks—is according to God's will. Since black theologians by their own insistence are concerned above all with a "liberation theology," that is, a theology which will help free blacks from oppression, their failure to deal with the white racist implications of their own theological premises amounts to a begging of the central question of theology.

One reason black theologians have not recognized the possibility of divine racism is that they have automatically accepted the traditional axiom that God is intrinsically good. Given this, whatever happens must somehow be good, if not intrinsically, then instrumentally. Within this framework, black theologians have struggled to identify some beneficent end served by black suffering. They simply do not take seriously the possibility that God may hate blacks and *wish* them to be oppressed.

Jones is not asserting that God is indeed a white racist, but only that given the presuppositions and conclusions generally accepted by black theologians these theologians cannot logically exclude divine racism as one plausible explanation of the suffering of blacks. If black theologians would grant this, they would then be in a position to question their own basic view of God and to consider whether it is really consistent with their own hopes and values. It is precisely this reconsideration of normative frameworks that Jones wishes to encourage.

Jones works toward this end by the method of internal criticism. He considers each of the various leading black theologies on its own terms, attempting by conceptual analysis to clarify its basic assumptions and logical demands. He then evaluates each system, not by reference to some absolute standard of truth, but in the light of its own principles. He asks whether internally the system is sufficiently coherent and well designed to be able to realize its own announced value commitments and social aspirations.

Internal criticism shows that black theology is seriously inadequate for the needs of black people. In their search for "prophetic enlightenment," Jones claims, the "current black theologians" have led the faithful down a road "full of logical potholes, theological washouts, and elaborate but unsound detours."[5] The chief cause of the trouble is "theocentric theism," a theological cosmology which all the leading black theologians favor. In this system, God possesses all wisdom and all power and controls the flow of history. Human beings look patiently to God, hoping for an auspicious resolution of their problems. This is unsatisfactory because it makes human beings overly dependent on God and weakens their impulse toward liberation. As long as people wait for God to act first, they will not feel the imperative to fight racism with all their strength; they will continue to deliver themselves into the hands of their oppressors under the illusion that they are trusting in the Lord.

Although Jones is anxious to help rebuild the theological

66

road, in this book he is content to identify the places that need repair and to lay the foundation for later construction. He describes his effort as a "prolegomenon to black theology." The new black theology should honor as its standard of theological adequacy the "functional ultimacy" of humanity. Blacks should accept no cosmology which does not give human beings full responsibility for their own affairs. Human beings must choose their values and goals, make their decisions, initiate and carry out their projects. Only in this kind of world is it likely that people will work fully for the liberation of the oppressed. Although a number of cosmologies allowing functional ultimacy are conceivable, Jones discusses only two as feasible alternatives to theocentric theism: "humanocentric theism," a world view which includes a God but focuses on human beings, and "secular humanism," an outlook which is neutral on the existence of God and focuses on human beings. Although Jones is personally inclined toward the latter, he regards the other as equally serviceable as a theoretical foundation for black thought and action since its views are basically consistent logically and meet the crucial functional ultimacy test. Jones opts for secular humanism because he has "not had the experience which authenticates to me the existence and/or goodness of God."[6] Jones does not urge his readers to become secular humanists, but he does invite the other black theologians, who presumably have had experiences which authenticate God to them, to move on from their traditional views to humanocentric theism. Internal criticism shows that many of the elements of humanocentric theism are already present in their current systems.

Directly, Jones is speaking to his fellow black theologians: James Cone, Major Jones, Joseph Washington, Albert Cleage, and J. Deotis Roberts; but, indirectly, he is speaking to all who are willing to face theological realities

67

and who prize consistency in their concept of God, especially to those who see the problem of suffering as the central theological issue. As I understand him, Jones agrees with the main contention of this book—that radical evil requires changes in the traditional idea of God's nature, not disbelief in God. As long as God is seen as sharing power with the creation and as giving human beings full responsibility for their own affairs, believing in God does not prevent humans from working for liberation. On the other hand, it is not clear whether Jones could accept the concept of God I have been urging, since he opposes any view in which God remains at the center of human concern and is creatively active in human affairs. Since within the secular humanist perspective human beings are to proceed as if there were no God, Jones seems to be saying that in the final analysis it makes no difference whether one believes in God or not, and this is very different from the position I have been advocating. We must, therefore, follow the high points of Jones's discussion and weigh his arguments carefully.

2. DIVINE RACISM

In order to make the traditionalist face the *possibility* of a demonic God, Jones launches a "frontal attack on the concept of God's *intrinsic* goodness." "The quickest and most effective way to execute this attack," he says, is to call attention to the "multievidentiality" of suffering. Multievidentiality "means that the same event points with equal validity toward opposing interpretations." Jesus' death on Calvary, for instance, has been interpreted by some as "God's crowning act of self-sacrificing love," but it has been interpreted by others—Camus, for example—as a pernicious strategem to justify suffering and cut the nerve of human rebellion against evil.[7] If Jesus Christ—who is both God and an exemplary human being—uncomplainingly bears the pain and injustice of the human condition, then every human being should do the same. Rebellion is quelled.

As Jones sees it, neither of these interpretations is more or less plausible than the other, for they both account for the observable facts of the Crucifixion. Which of them is true depends on God's motive, and since no human being can confidently claim to know even another human being's motive, much less God's, there is no way to know what the point of the Crucifixion is. All we can do is what we do in determining motives in the human sphere, namely, infer them from behavior. We "look at the individual's actual behavior and then argue backward to a prior motive."[8] As Sartre teaches, every human being is the sum of his acts. Applying this existentialist principle, we must say that God, like any other agent, is what he does. He, too, is the sum of his acts.

How has God acted toward blacks? The record speaks for itself: God has subjected blacks to a prolonged, destructive, and unmerited life of suffering. The responsibility for this cannot be diverted from God to human beings, for on traditionalist assumptions, God is sovereign in the world he has created.

Nor will Jones accept the excuse that God will compensate blacks in the next life. This attributes to God an intention which is inconsistent with his actions in this world, and this, in turn, violates the principle that God is the sum of his acts. Moreover, Jones notes, the appeal to eschatological deliverance is not authentically biblical. Biblical eschatology looks toward a corrective development in the course of human history, something which can be pointed to here and now as a precursor of the radically changed situation to come. Since the present and past history of blacks is oppression, this precursory element is missing. If we anticipate the future in terms of the past and present, blacks can expect nothing but more of the same.

Sooner or later, Jones contends, the appeal to an eschatological resolution of suffering ends in an "unresolved mystery" which tries to balance "a known suffering, an actual event, with an anticipated event whose actuality and commensurate quality are both problematical." It is, in effect, a "theodicy of last resort," which requires that we accept things as they are and, like Camus's priest, Paneloux, either love God or hate God, blindly.[9]

Jones is equally skeptical of efforts to defend God's benevolence toward blacks on grounds that they are God's suffering servants and thus are secretly enwrapped in God's love. Again, the evidence does not unequivocally support this. In the Bible God always at some point uplifts his suffering servants in an "exaltation event," some extraordinary occurrence which discloses their special status and reassures them that in spite of their pain they are its beloved. The Jews were delivered from Egypt; Jesus was resurrected. No such gloriously compensating, confirming event is seen in black history. There is only the dreary, crushing experience of oppression and more oppression.[10] In short, the usual ways of defending God's benevolence prove sadly unconvincing, and the charge of divine racism remains unrefuted.

Jones takes special care to identify the points at which each of the leading black theologians opens the door to divine racism, and he discovers that in every case it is some facet of the theocentric view of God which is at fault. In one way or another, all of these theologians maintain that God, being omnipotent, is able to end black suffering but for some allegedly benevolent reason wants it to continue.

Unfortunately, what they do not see is that God's reason for wishing blacks to suffer might be that he hates blacks, and the reason they do not see this is that they assume uncritically that God is *inherently* benevolent.

Although black theologians have thus inadvertently allowed themselves to become entangled in racist doctrines, Jones thinks they have the potential to break free and go on to genuine liberationist positions. All of them claim for human beings a relatively active role in the struggle for freedom. Blacks are to protest and oppose the oppressors; they are to fight with God against injustice. In this the black theologians are straining against the limits of their theocentric assumptions and reaching for some alternative cosmology which will give human beings a more determinative role in their own history. Jones, of course, is glad of this and hopeful that his colleagues will move on to either humanocentric theism or secular humanism.

3. GOD IN HUMANOCENTRIC THEISM AND SECULAR HUMANISM

Since it is the nature of God and its relation to humankind that carries the racist implications in theocentric theism, let us consider what humanocentric theism and secular humanism offer as a corrective. As an alternative to traditional Christianity, Jones turns to the neglected humanist strand of black religion, whose representatives have not been convinced that God is righteous, just, and loving, and who have protested in the name of suffering blacks against God itself. Jones quotes one of these, the poet Countee Cullen, who speculates in his poem "Color" on the reasons for black suffering. Dissatisfied with conventional explanations, Cullen proposes that it may be that (1) "there is no God, i.e., atheism," (2) "God exists but is not active in human affairs," or (3) "God exists and is active in certain sectors of human history but absents himself from the struggle for black liberation."[11] Any of these alternatives, Jones suggests, can explain black suffering as logically as theocentric theism.

Jones introduces these options not because he thinks that they exhaust all likely alternatives to theocentric theism but because they have seemed plausible to black humanists and because they provide useful guidelines for the fresh thinking which Jones wishes to stimulate. Clearly, his own alternatives of humanocentric theism and secular humanism are formulated with Cullen's three possibilities in the background. Humanocentric theism seems to be an example of the second possibility, and secular humanism points to a fourth possibility which Cullen does not mention, namely, that there may or may not be a God, and in either case there is insufficient evidence to say that God is active in the struggle for black liberation. This would add an agnostic alternative, something for the person who says: "I do not know about the existence of God, but I do know from the apparent neutrality and randomness of the world that human beings must carry the responsibility for their own lives. The existence of a supreme being guarantees nothing—neither victory nor defeat. Injustice occurs because human beings perpetrate it, and it can be stopped if human beings will stop it."

Since Jones feels personally unable either to affirm or deny the existence of God, he cannot reject any of Cullen's three possibilities as untrue, nor can he accept them. He would seem to be obliged to declare for agnosticism and to remain neutral toward all the others. On what basis, then, does he give humanocentric theism (Cullen's third category) a special status as the leading candidate other than his own? Does he compare all the alternatives according to

72

their ability to generate a vigorous and persevering opposition to oppression and endorse humanocentric theism and secular humanism because they can do this best? That is, should we read Jones as a pragmatist on this point?

Since Jones is clearly interested in action and results, this is tempting; however, as far as I know, he nowhere actually offers such reasoning. What he actually does is invoke the test of consistency. Which cosmology is more consistent with the concepts of God, humanity, and value that blacks espouse? Which cosmology will encourage blacks to take an initiating role in their own liberation and thus lead most directly to overcoming oppression? The answer is that on all these counts humanocentric theism and secular humanism are superior. Atheism and deism (Cullen's first and second possibilities, respectively) no doubt cohere with the values and religious beliefs of *some* persons concerned with human liberation and are best for them; but they are not best for most blacks—at least not for the current body of leading black theologians.

Given Jones's agnosticism, this seems plausible enough; and yet there is something curious about this simultaneous acceptance of two such different world views. How can a world *with* a God and a world *without* a God be equally consistent with the values and other theological commitments of blacks? Such contradictory positions surely must carry some significantly different implications.

An explanation comes if we consider Jones's position first as theory, then as practice. As theory, it is plainly agnostic. He has not had the experiences which would verify God for him, and therefore he does not affirm God; yet neither does he deny that others have had such experiences and are entitled to affirm God. He is equally open to both positions. At the practical level, however, Jones leans the other way. It is the practical absence of God in both humanocentric theism and secular humanism which attracts him. Whether we believe in God or not, within these positions we do not look for God to *do* anything. This is what makes it possible for human beings to be functionally ultimate, and this, remember, is Jones's criterion for theological adequacy. That God does nothing in secular humanism is obvious, since secular humanism explicitly proposes a world without God; but this is also true in humanocentric theism even though it envisions the world with God.

The God of humanocentric theism does no more in the world of humankind than if it did not exist at all. Consider the essential traits of this cosmology as Jones presents it. Humanocentric theism is a world in which (1) by God's "purpose and plan" human beings enjoy "an exalted status," with full recognition of their freedom; (2) God creates human beings as "co-determining" centers of power with himself and in so doing gives the "most authentic expression of his sovereignty"; (3) the highest human good is conceived as a process which stresses human activity and choice; (4) God gives human beings such independence of himself that they are functionally ultimate relative to their own history; and (5) God's omnipotence is redefined to "fit the requirements of the freedom of God *and* man," this being understood in terms of God's benevolence in granting this freedom.[12] In sum, humanocentric theism is like secular humanism in that it conceives the world as a place in which human beings—because of the absence of God—are completely responsible for their own lives and destinies. The fourth feature above is the crucial one. God stays out of the critical events of human history; in Jones's words, God is "functionally neutral relative to human affairs."[13]

Thus, in Jones's estimate, both humanocentric theism and secular humanism are forms of practical atheism, by

74

which I mean that people following these ways act as if God does not exist whether they believe in God or not. Jones's functional ultimacy principle explicitly requires such behavior: "man must act *as if* he were the ultimate valuator or the ultimate agent in human history or both."[14] Human beings who function as ultimate agents in these respects exclude God from their lives no matter what they say with their lips. The point is that as long as Jones's functional ultimacy criterion of theological validity prevails, humanocentric theism and secular humanism are, practically speaking, indistinguishable.

At one point Jones states this explicitly. Referring to something of humanocentric theism which this author discussed in an earlier book, Jones says "there is no significant difference between his [Burkle's] variety of theism, on the one hand, and atheism or humanism on the other."[15] That Jones can say this in spite of the fact that the book to which he refers is a sustained argument for God as a persuading participant in history, implies that Jones sees the God of humanocentric theism as a gratuity, a halfway house for those who have been cured of dependency on the theocentric God but who are not yet resolved to live entirely on their own.

This concerns me greatly, since there is much in humanocentric theism which I accept. As long as human dignity and creativity are seen as deriving from God's aboriginal gift and as having been sustained by God's continuing participation in our present endeavors, I am quite willing to accept this label. However, I do not consider it necessary or desirable to endorse Jones's atheistic reading of the position. On the contrary, I wish to argue that because of God humanocentric theism is, in certain ways, very different from secular humanism. In humanocentric theism, God is active in human history. God offers cosmic support for every constructive venture, particularly for conflict situations such as the struggle for black liberation. I believe that this makes a difference in the way people think and feel, what they expect, and how they behave. In short, I wish to argue that Jones is right in urging us to break out of the constraints of traditionalist theocentric theism, but wrong in thinking that this requires the practical exclusion of God.

4. THE INTRINSIC GOODNESS OF GOD

I agree with the general intent of Jones's multi-evidentiality argument; human experience is indeed highly ambiguous and open to various interpretations. However, I do not agree that the evidence points toward opposing conclusions of equal validity. I have opted for a benevolent God and am engaged in explaining why I think that this choice is justified by the evidence. I have conceded that my judgment is no doubt shaped by my prior commitments. I already believe in God and cannot simply cease believing for methodological purposes. Thus, inevitably my procedure has been to seek to reconcile God's goodness with the radical evils which seem to belie it. Although it seems to me that the explanations offered thus far do vindicate belief in God, I do not, and in the nature of the case cannot, know whether I would have come to my present position if I had started with a neutral outlook and depended on nothing but a preponderance of positive evidence to convince me. I have tried to look openly at the negative evidence; indeed, I would claim that I have been using Jones's method of "counterevidence," whereby one gives "careful, deliberate, and sympathetic consideration" to the position opposing one's own and tries to build a theological "framework capable of accommodating" the contradictory materials.[16] In the concepts of divine self-limitation and co-creatorship advanced earlier I think I have offered the necessary framework and shown that the evidence points more strongly toward than away from God.

Before we can move to state the case for theism, however, we must face Jones's crucial contention that God may be demonic, a supernatural Dr. Jekyl and Mr. Hyde. It seems to me that this very idea is inherently inconsistent and therefore not a possibility at all. God cannot be demonic because "God" means "absolute perfection." If the dominant universal power is not *perfectly* good, there is no God. Atheism is the truth, and the human world is governed or dominated by a nondivine force or forces which, from the human point of view, are in some ways antithetical, in some ways helpful, in some ways indifferent. Whether one is attracted to humanocentric theism, secular humanism, atheism, a modified form of theocentric theism, or some other cosmology, the basic choice is the stark alternative between (1) no God, or (2) a *perfectly* good God ("perfectly good" is redundant here, but I state it to avoid confusion).

If this is so, some of the alternatives Jones considers are incoherent and thus are not genuine possibilities. This is the case with (1) an *omnipotent* benevolent God, (2) an indifferent God, (3) an uninvolved God, and (4) a malevolent God. Enough has been said already to show why the first (traditional theocentric theism) is incoherent. What needs to be recognized is that the second, third, and fourth possibilities are also incoherent, because in one way or another they contradict the criterion of perfect goodness. None of these "Gods" is "that being than which no greater can be conceived." A God who is indifferent to its creatures' suffering lacks appropriate concern for value. A God who does not participate in all its creatures' struggles against oppression is not fully creative. A malevolent God is not a creator but a destroyer. The four alternatives are all forms of atheism, and therefore the root cosmological choice is (1) no God or (2) God understood as perfectly benevolent and appropriately limited in power.

It might be objected that it is arbitrary to be unwilling to call an indifferent, an uninvolved, or a malevolent supreme power God. Why is it not legitimate to define God as whatever possesses predominating power, regardless of its moral qualities or its disposition toward human beings? If this is done, all of Cullen's and Jones's cosmological possibilities, which I have just ruled incoherent, would regain their legitimacy.

All persons are, of course, free to define God as they see fit, and if the definitions seem fitting, so be it. All we can do is reflect on our definitions and ask whether they can be justified. I do not see how human beings can address anything or anyone as God that is not worthy of reverence, worship, and obedience. I believe that we all naturally hunger for the supremely good. We enjoy the goods we can attain and look beyond them questingly to further goods. The idea of God arises in us in this process as the good which cannot be transcended and which forever satisfies. All of us have at least the potentiality of an idea of this good, of that being than which no greater can be conceived. We may never have reflected seriously on it, or we may have reflected at length and come to doubt that there is any reality answering to it, or we may believe with all our heart that there is such a reality. However, we all know that only this being is properly called God. If we are thinking of a good which lacks any *possible* goodness, it cannot be God. It is, therefore, impossible that human beings could be objects of *divine* hatred or indifference.[17]

5. THE STRENGTH OF A SELF-LIMITED GOD

The concept of divine limitation developed in connection with the Holocaust applies to racism as well. Although everything that occurs in the world follows directly or indirectly from God's will, not everything that occurs conforms to God's wishes. God does not wish that any creature should suffer unjustly or excessively. However, when God endowed some creatures with freedom and a high degree of creative potential, it necessarily endowed them with a high degree of destructive potential also. God opened the door to the possibility—indeed, the virtual certainty—that unjust and excessive evil would occur. God could have elected not to create this world, and when it defied its will, God could have destroyed it or radically altered it by retracting the grant of freedom; but one thing that God could not do was have a world containing free creatures who are unable to choose.

Thus, racism comes not from God's hatred but from humanity's misdirection of its God-given creative-destructive energy. Admittedly, it is God who has made us capable of hating. However, this is not because God wishes us to hate, but because it wishes us to choose to love. Also, admittedly, it is God who has made destruction possible. Again, however, this is not because God wants destruction to occur, but because it wants all creatures capable of choice to *choose* to live creatively. Racism represents a tragic miscarriage of God's intentions.

Although divine powerlessness poses serious dangers, it also opens up possibilities of goodness which otherwise would be foreclosed. In limiting its own power and thus exposing the creation and itself to great destructivity, God enables us to perform acts of great ingenuity and heroism. God's acceptance of self-imposed limits increases manyfold the significance of everything human beings do. We can be vastly worse and vastly better than ever we could be in a more tightly controlled world. This is to say, God's powerlessness is a condition of *divine-human* creativity. If God can persuade us to forgo our destructive tendencies and apply our energies to beneficent ends, God will have created an incomparably rich new reality. If God does finally fully win our love, it will have carried through one of the greatest of all possible projects and proved itself as powerful as reason and goodness allow. Perhaps we might even say that God will have shown itself omnipotent in the *true* sense—as having accomplished the very most that love and wisdom can accomplish, while respecting the rights and fully employing the contributions of all finite co-creators.

There are other positive implications of a self-limited God. Such a view can do much to avoid quietism. It can do this not only because it places responsibility for the cure of human problems on human shoulders but because it surrounds human beings with an ambience of divine excitation which encourages us to deal with our problems. Needing our help, God appeals to us to use our ambivalent life energies constructively. God presents to our intellects myriads of possible values and confronts our consciences with goals graded for relevance and usefulness. Offering but never fully giving itself, God leads us constantly toward better conditions. It is difficult to imagine a cosmology better able to elicit vigorous, free human activity than this one founded in a God who is itself loving and just and who calls on all free creatures to be loving and just, too.

Would not the same effect be secured in a cosmology in which there is no God at all? Indeed, would not there be even more urgency toward good if God were eliminated entirely and the total responsibility for ameliorative effort were placed on human beings alone? From what I understand of human motivation, I should say no. If there is no God, to the universe it is a matter of small importance whether racism is eliminated. Whether racism disappears or remains depends on what human beings want, and the fact is that many human beings—some of the most powerfully and strategically placed—want racism. Those who wish to eliminate racism have to struggle not only with racism as an objective problem but with themselves and other human beings. The very ones who must act if racism is to be eliminated are themselves suffering from the ailment in a way which weakens their will to act.

In short, human beings cannot carry so much responsibility alone. We need support from beyond ourselves. We need an encouraging context in which to act. We need evidence that our efforts to change the world are congruent with reality at its deepest level. We need something in the world beyond us, as well as within our own consciences, to assure us that our dreams of equality, justice, and community are not just private fantasies. We need the pressure of an independent moral imperative to help us persevere when the struggle becomes too much for us. We need a universal ideal drawing from us more than what at any given moment we are capable of giving. We need a compassionate Spirit who knows what we have done and have not done, who can forgive us and help us acknowledge, renounce, and forget our sins. We need a cosmic companion who links us not only to others who are likeminded, but to our opponents, whom we seek not to destroy but to change. In short, we need God.

This is why I have maintained that it is not all the same whether we adopt humanocentric theism or secular humanism. These are two very different universes. If we are humanists, we and the few persons who share our values are alone, with nothing but our own ingenuity and

81

courage to sustain us. We hope that the cosmos does not despise our values, but we have no assurance that it favors them. If, like Jones, we identify with an existentialist sort of humanism,[18] we cannot even take consolation in the *rightness* of our values, for there are no objective rights and wrongs. If we are theists, however, we visualize ourselves in immediate relation to God and to all other human beings whether or not they share our passion for justice. We live in the faith that there are objective values and fulfilling goals and that when we pursue these, the cosmos supports us. We see it as our responsibility to do all we can to bring ourselves and our world into line with these God-given norms.

This is why I cannot accept Jones's interpretation of the following passage he quotes from my earlier book, that "pragmatically speaking, believing in a persuading God and believing in no God at all come to very much the same thing."[19] Jones interprets this statement as saying that our relation to a persuading God makes no practical difference at all. This is not what I intended, although I see now that my words invite that construction. What I should have said is that with respect to the crucial matter of what human beings contribute to the constructive work of the world, there is no difference between believing in a persuading God and believing in none at all. In both cases, unless human beings act, the work does not get done. Moreover, as in secular humanism, human beings are irreducibly responsible for what they do. They must conceive and carry out whatever is done.

Nevertheless, there are crucial differences. Believers do all of this in a personal context. They do it with and before the God who wills the well-being of all creatures. Believers see their possibilities of choice as deriving from God, as making spiritual-moral claims, as inspiring our action; and most important of all, believers perceive their every constructive action to be actively supported and approved by the very deepest level of reality. They imagine that the small goods they do are augmented and preserved by an undercurrent of divine goodness.

Although I have expressed a qualified approval of the designation "humanocentric theism," I must reject the connotation some may find in the term that the *universe* centers in human beings. Surely this puerile idea deserves to be rejected. Human concerns, which seem infinitely important to us, are often but local turbulences in the vast sweep and complexity of the universe. Not even human affairs center entirely in human beings. In the cosmology I am supporting, human existence is valuable in its own right and in the eyes of God, but it centers in God, who is the source, ground, and goal of all things. Although God unceasingly draws us toward the center and gives us significance, God is the true center. Even when we are most active and self-reliant, God the persuader leads. It is God who presents the possibilities, and weights their relevance, who desires the good and sets a climate which encourages others to desire it too, who ultimately accepts and preserves whatever we do and shares with us the bitter or joyous consequences. It is God's beauty which draws our attention beyond ourselves and enables us to escape parochial, partisan, and merely expediential interests.

Although I have argued that we ought to accept a persuading God because doing so carries invaluable benefits, what I wish to emphasize is that, strictly speaking, there is no coherent alternative. God *must* work by persuasion. It cannot just give free beings a perfect world to begin with and cannot reconstruct this world by fiat; and the reason is that these things *cannot be done*. Not even the omnipotent deity of tradition, who (as Luther puts it) "can do, and does . . . 'whatever he wills in heaven and earth,' " can do the intrinsically impossible. To think that God can actually do whatever we confusedly speak of or vaguely imagine is the stuff of fantasy, magic, self-indulgence. I submit that a moment's reflection on the meaning of racism will show that racism cannot be instantaneously banished except by banishing the human agents who perpetrate it.

I suppose that when people ask why God does not intervene and rectify the harmful consequences of human choice, they have in mind analogies like the following: a mother steps between her quarreling children and restrains their blows, a lad pulls his brother out of the path of an approaching auto, rain begins to fall on a parched garden. Such direct, dramatic, salvific interventions do sometimes occur. Mere human beings do them, mere nature produces them; why cannot God, the very Lord of the universe, do the like? Does not Exodus tell us that something like this occurred at the Red Sea?

Jones, quite plainly, is willing to countenance such an idea of divine power, for he attributes it to traditional theism and takes that cosmology to task because of it. In traditional theism, says Jones, quoting Cullen, "Jesus' power is unmistakable . . . in his victory over death."[20] In this "exaltation-event" (the Resurrection), God shows that it possesses the power to rescue those who suffer and punish those who inflict suffering. Note: God's power over life and death is cited as evidence of its power over the human spirit. Just as God can step in and reverse the natural processes of organic disintegration, so it can step in and reverse the thought processes, value commitments, and decisions of free agents. An omnipotent being can do anything.

I am aware that at this juncture Jones is exploring the implications of the traditional black doctrine of God rather than stating his own. Nevertheless, he treats this idea of divine power as if it were coherent. He does not protest the very concept of an omnipotent controller of human choice, and this is what is called for. There is a categorical difference between God's doing something which does not require a personal response (as in creating the world or resurrecting a human being) and its doing something which does require a human response (as in asking a person to make a decision). That God has power to do the first does not imply that it has the power to do the second. It is not contradictory—however incredible it may seem—to say that God at appropriate times makes natural processes do what they cannot naturally do, but it is contradictory to say that God makes *free* agents do what they do not elect to do. Not even the tragic centuries of black suffering and the desperate need to have suffering terminated can make the impossible possible. God cannot end racism by fiat because it cannot be done; and it cannot be done because the act we think we are imagining is nonsense. A compelled free being is no more an imaginable, realizable entity than a round square.

I do not doubt that some will think that a God so limited is too high a price for freedom. Some will say that if in creating this human race God had to allow for the possibility of four hundred years of oppression for blacks, for the torture and murder of six million Jews, and for countless other acts of outrage and insult against every kind of human being, it ought not to have created the world—better no world than this one. Or, the critic might say, it would have been better if God had created another kind of human being, one with less destructive potency.

This proposal may sound reasonable and promising. If the human species is defective because of its vast power to destroy, let God modify it. However, I am convinced that this alternative is confused and in the final analysis impracticable. How would God modify human nature? Would it simply make us unable to perform destructive acts? In that case we could choose which creative acts to perform but not whether to choose creatively. We would be technicians, automatons in carrying out God's will, and not free beings in the fullest sense. Moreover, the proposal asks that God create a humanity *innately* endowed with wisdom, love of justice, concern for others, and control over its own decision-making powers; that is, it is calling not for a modified humanity, but for an essentially different kind of being. The proposal is tacitly misanthropic. It says that God ought not to have created the being we know as human, that God erred tragically in bringing forth a race who are so precariously balanced between good and evil, who can become wise only by outgrowing folly, who can achieve some degree of selflessness only after tasting the bitterness of greed—in short—who can become truly human only through their own efforts.

I do not find it self-evident that such misanthropy is wrong. The black parents who have such thoughts after seeing their children brutalized by racists have every right to question whether the human species deserves to exist; and if they decide that it does not, I cannot blame them. We have only as much light as we can find in the place where we are, and I have never stood where a grieving black parent stands. I can only say from where I am that I would rather there be human beings, with all their flaws, than some divinely programmed doers of good. Moreover, I think that others, in their quieter moments, agree with me, that even when in their sorrow they call for the radical rejection of human freedom they do so in the name of a human nature which includes that freedom. It is partly because the black parents so value their children as potentially creative beings that they might call upon God to remove the destructive powers from human nature. But this is an act of last resort, born of desperation. Although I can understand why someone would ask for this, I cannot but think that if it were granted, humanity would have suffered its greatest and final tragedy.

It seems to me that the inherent worthiness of human beings is so apparent to us all—at least when we are looking upon those who are close to us, whom we can easily accept as our own—that we cannot ultimately desire that the human race as we know it did not exist. We do not in our deepest hearts believe that God erred in creating us. What we want is that the nature God gave us be perfected, that its energies be formed and directed in creative channels, that its innate inexperience, ignorance, and egocentricity be restructured. However, this is not something which can be attained in a flash by God's acting directly on human agents. It can only be achieved by human agents responding lovingly and intelligently to God's lead. It can come, and when it does we shall at last cleanse the earth of racism.

CHAPTER 4

SUPPRESSION

1. BEYOND GOD THE FATHER

The last of the dimensions of absurdity which we must consider is the suppression of women, for in sheer quantitative terms—number and distribution of victims and temporal extent of suffering—the suppression of women is certainly the most far-reaching and perhaps the most heinous of all the forms of absurdity that human beings inflict on other human beings. As theologian and women's liberationist Mary Daly says, "There exists a worldwide phenomenon of sexual caste, basically the same whether one lives in Saudi Arabia or in Sweden . . . [that] involves birth-ascribed hierarchically ordered groups whose members have unequal access to goods, services, and prestige and to physical and mental well-being."[1]

Indeed, if Mary Daly is correct, sexism is also *qualitatively* the most destructive of all evils. It is not only one of the evils but part of the soil from which the others grow. Consider the "Most Unholy Trinity" of rape, genocide, and war, which Daly thinks are the chief evils of the world today. All of them stem from sexist attitudes toward women. Rape obviously does so. War, too, is basically an expression of misogynistic impulses directed not only at women but at the whole of another society. Observe how often in the moment of military conquest the victorious soldiers rape the women of the vanquished group, thus revealing their motivation. Genocide also is misogynism. What went on in the Nazi death camps was the infliction of male sexual violence on a helpless minority group. The murder of millions of Jews was essentially group enactment of the "primordial act of violation," which German males first learned as a way of dealing with females.[2]

Suppression has profound theological significance, for it seems to belie all the traditional assertions about the power and goodness of God. How can one believe that history is guided by a just and powerful God when women are locked into a world which negates their full worth and denies them access to the resources which would enable them to develop their full potentials? How can one accept the proposition that God is love when women everywhere are demeaned or despised, or are degraded by specious adulation? Clearly, something is wrong not only in the society which perpetuates these injuries but in the theology which provides their rationale. As a result, more women than ever before are questioning or rejecting the God of traditional Western theology.

Mary Daly's *Beyond God the Father* is a leading statement of the case against the traditional God, and we shall review the highlights of her discussion in order to have the basic issues before us. Daly's protest strikes at the "symbol of the Father God," the "great patriarch in heaven," which "has dominated the imagination of millions over thousands of years."[3]

This idea of God has generated many forms of fanatical and inhuman behavior. Whenever it is taken seriously, it reduces human beings to a position of "infantile subjection" and makes them fit objects for exploitation. It puts believers at odds with unbelievers and turns true believers against dissenters and heretics. Most destructive of all, it leads to the suppression of women. "If God in 'his' heaven is a father ruling 'his' people, then it is in the 'nature' of things and according to divine plan and the order of the universe that society be male-dominated."[4] In the name of God the Father, males dominate females. The resulting warped social system then projects the male supremacist values into the realm of dogma and uses them to justify and conserve the system. It treats any denial of male dominance as infidelity to God. The result is a vicious circle in which the Father God and human injustice support each other and powerfully resist change.[5]

Another facet of Daly's basic objection to the Father God concept is that it gives an artificially polarized picture of maleness and femaleness. The male, conceived in God's image, is hyper-rational, objective, aggressive, manipulative toward persons and the environment, and inclined to draw boundaries between himself and "the Other" (those who are not identified with his group). Women are the opposite. They are: hyperemotional, passive, and self-abnegating—everything males are not and, of course, everthing which tends to keep them perpetually in their subjugated place in society.[6]

Daly identifies the ways in which theologians and religious leaders use the idea of the Father God against women. They may declare openly that it is God's will that women be subordinate to men. Or they may speak of God in "one-sex" symbolism so that women, constantly hearing God referred to as "he" and human beings as "men," will feel themselves strangers and less than human.[7]Or they may represent God as detached from the human struggle against oppression. Christians and others who accept the Father God notion have again and again done these things. Even "sophisticated thinkers . . . [who] have never *intellec-tually* identified God with a Superfather in heaven"

world necessarily demeans and in some sense oppresses all its creatures, human and nonhuman, female and male. It is this *kind* of God and the social patterns and human attitudes that it causes which are the targets of her anger.[10]

What is the nature of the God Daly would substitute for the Father God? First, let us be clear what it is not. Certainly, God is not male. Moreover, God is not two other qualities which Daly associates with maleness—neither a distinct being (entity) separate from the world, nor a superintending agent who manipulates the world according to its will. Also, God is not a "stop-gap for the incompleteness of our knowledge," nor an "otherworldly" Reality which draws our attention away from this world with promises of life to come, nor a "Judge of 'sin' " who confirms the "rules and roles of the reigning system" and maintains "false consciences and self-destructive guilt feelings."[11]

What of Daly's positive assertions about God? Everything she says in description of God is tested by a "pragmatic yardstick or verification process." She is interested primarily in what God *does.* She looks to results as the clues to what God *is,* and she will accept only qualities which contribute to liberation. "Does this language [about God] hinder human becoming by reinforcing sex-role socialization?" If so, it is not true of God. "Does it *encourage* human becoming toward psychological and social fulfillment, toward an androgynous mode of living, toward transcendence?" If so, it can tell us something about God.[12]

Thus, Daly's theology is liberation theology. It is talk about God as that Reality which facilitates the liberation of women and, through them, all human beings. To liberate is to enable those whose potential is blocked by unjust or inauspicious conditions to become really open to the future and to achieve and sustain self-transcendence. The basic positive statement is that God is that Reality which stimulates human creativity and actualizes human potential.

This does not mean that God *acts upon* human beings to make them into what they become, for that is precisely the sort of paternalistic manipulation Daly is combating. Daly's God offers fresh possibilities and encourages humanity to choose well, but at the same time it allows human beings to shape their own lives. God's not *doing* anything to others has the effect of strengthening human power to act. God creates by allowing others to create.

Although this might seem a passive sort of God, Daly intends just the opposite. In fact, she suggests that God be thought of not as a noun but as a verb—"the most active and dynamic of all . . . in which we participate—live, move, and have our being." This "Verb of Verbs" is active but intransitive. As we have said, it does not do anything to anyone else. It is "Be-ing"—power so dynamic that just by existing it empowers others to become more fully themselves.[13] Daly uses Tillich's term the "power of being" to speak of God as that in which all finite beings participate and from which they, so to speak, draw their power to be.

Be-ing, then, is better thought of as Process or Becoming than as Being. Daly describes it as "a power of being which both is, and is not yet." In another place, she speaks of God as perpetually "unfolding," that is, actualizing its potentialities.[14] God is the model of what human beings spiritually should be. This is why God can support the creative efforts of others; its own creativity provides an atmosphere which nourishes and reinforces other creators, particularly those who, like women, are striving to overcome obstacles and become what they essentially are capable of being. In moving toward androgynous being, women—and those men who respond positively to the divine invitation to liberation—participate in the unfolding of God. Indeed, God's unfolding in part consists in its creatures' actualizations. Human beings, as William James has said, help perfect God; they enrich the very divine being itself.[15]

It might be thought that this God—however inspiring—is impersonal, but Daly denies it. Human beings, in their "creative potential" are in the "image of God" and thus are clues to what God is.[16] This is not to say that God is like a human person. It is "not necessary to anthropomorphize or reify transcendence in order to relate to this personally."[17] It is to say that the act of self-transcendence by which we relate to the unfolding God is personalizing. By naming ourselves toward the unnamed God, we discover the hidden God which lies beyond female and male and supports our personhood. "What is perceived in this new way of being is the Eternal Thou, the creative divine word that always has *more* to say to us."[18]

3. GOD AS ACTIVITY

It has often been observed that it is not those who suffer most who deny God. "How strange," says Elie Wiesel, "that the philosophy denying God came not from the survivors" of the Holocaust.[19] It is not those who faced the crematory fires but some of those who were forced to look on in horror from afar who now deny God. The vast majority of Jewish spokesmen, although staggered by what has happened to their people, continue to hold fast to the God of history. As William R. Jones tells us, a similar condition prevails within the U. S. black community. In spite of all that blacks have endured, the majority of black theologians hold firmly to the traditional view of the biblical God.

Do we find this pattern repeated in the feminist theology of Mary Daly? In one respect, we do indeed. In spite of her

94

spirited and uncompromising attack on God the Father, she does not repudiate God as such. She insists that women's liberation depends on their keeping alive the question of God and actualizing their potential within the matrix of a divine becoming which nurtures and incorporates all becoming within itself.

In other respects, however, Daly breaks out of the traditionalist pattern. There is none of the ambivalence and hesitancy one sees in Fackenheim; she does not urge women to pray softly to God lest they be heard. She considers it vital that women be heard by God. She is convinced that God has nothing to do with the violation of women but rather encourages and supports women's efforts towards self-actualization. She sees belief in God not as a liability or a seemingly irrational legacy of tradition but as a positive, necessary step toward deliverance—salvation, if you will. Also, Daly differs from the leading black theologians in critical ways. She goes further in removing from God the qualities like omnipotence, omniscience, and efficient causality by which God is supposed to exercise absolute control over history. Moreover, Daly looks to human beings, and especially to women, for the deeds which can both change the course of human affairs for the better and effect the liberation of the oppressed.

The becoming of women may be not only the doorway to deliverance which secular humanism has passionately sought for—but also a doorway *to* something, that is, a new phase in the human spirit's quest for God. . . . I am suggesting that at this point in history women are in a unique sense called to be the bearers of existential courage in society.[20]

In this, she fits very well into William R. Jones's category of humanocentric theism, and she also confirms my conviction that God can accomplish its aims for the human race only through human beings. Human courage is the fulcrum of divine creativity in human history.

Accordingly, I accept enthusiastically many of Daly's revisions, particularly her campaign to expunge paternalistic qualities from our concept of God. God must not be thought of as male, white, Christian, or any other quality which gives an advantage to any class of human beings. It is not enough to refrain from using male personal pronouns when referring to human beings generally; we must also not use them of God. This is awkward for a Christian not only because Jesus addressed God as "Father" but also because if we do not use personal pronouns of God, we seem to have no alternative language except either the vacuous neuter "it" or some sex-neutral neologism which is not likely to mean much to those who hear it. I have used "it" here, not because I think it ideal, but because it at least blunts the bias toward maleness and, all things considered, is less unsatisfactory than any alternative I know. Perhaps in time theologians can develop a terminology for referring to God which draws upon all good qualities—male, female, neuter, and androgynous—which are expressive of the valid parental concern which Jesus was trying to convey in the "Father" image.

The persistence of belief in God among those persons who have suffered most seems to support the point I have been arguing from the beginning. Not even prolonged, intense, and unmerited suffering must undermine commitment to a God who is creatively involved in the world. On the contrary, it should strengthen it. If thoughtful, perceptive blacks, Jews, and women—people who know great suffering from within, existentially—generally continue to believe in God because of what they have experienced and are still experiencing, then surely there must be good reasons for doing so. So many persons of such quality cannot be merely obstinate and afraid of change.

Moreover, if we scrutinize what those who suffer most from absurdity are saying about the God they persist in affirming, we may notice a certain convergence of meaning. Although they differ over whether God is an entity and "does" anything in and to the world, they agree that God is, quite properly, limited in power. God's power in the human sphere lies in the constructive projects it can induce human beings to take on voluntarily. God gives, acknowledges, and nurtures the independence and potency of the beings of the world and cooperates with them in pursuit of their mutual objectives.

What we can learn from a creative encounter with absurdity, I think, is that what needs changing is not our believing in God but some aspects of our ideas about what God is. We need to be more rigorous and insistent in our acceptance of the principle that God is Love. We must reject any divine attribute which implies or encourages the suppression of human beings or the violation of the natural environment. We may be sure that if any aspect of our idea of God results in suppression, that attribute is a projection of our own disorder and is no part of God. I believe that human beings have an innate and virtually inextinguishable sense of rightness about this—about what is fair and humane—and thus about what God essentially is. Also, we need to elevate radically our own understanding of what it means to say that God is that being than which no greater can be conceived. We *know* that God cannot be willingly involved in anything which degrades or destroys and can only work for the preservation and enhancement of every manner and form of positive value.

In the concept of divine persuasion, I have been supporting a principle that should have this positive effect.

In my discussion of Camus's humanistic absurdism, I spoke of a God who is active throughout the world and involved in all human affairs—not a God who reserves itself for those who are "religious" or privileged to be in charge of the sacred precincts. God is not just what the religious people say. In confronting the Holocaust I spoke of a God who cares for Jews in a special sense and for all other groups in ways which are special to them. God is not just what Jews, Christians, Muslims, Buddhists, or Hindus say. In examining racism I spoke of a God who grieves over the oppression of blacks and who is working constantly for them and all others who are oppressed. God is not just what whites or blacks say. In this chapter on female suppression I wish to affirm a God who sides with women and participates in their struggle against the system which thwarts their basic drive toward fulfillment. God is not just what men say. The God of persuasion is with all human beings everywhere, working incessantly to check the forces of destruction, to heal those who are injured, and to coax into full activity those energies which have been blocked.

Since many of the qualities of the Father God contradict persuasion, Daly's critique of this concept is entirely justified, and many of her suggestions for revising it are well taken. However, some of her suggested changes are mistaken, I think. Why is it wrong to think of God as an entity? There is no necessary connection between God's being an entity and its manipulating and controlling the world as a mere object. This would depend on the *sort* of entity God is and how God relates to others. As Buber (whose ideas Daly evidently admires) explains, God and other personal beings can speak the "I-Thou" word, that is, by their mode of presenting themselves, bring into being an intensely personal society in which each being participates in the being of others without losing its own being. The

98

persons who relate themselves in this way, who become thou's for other thou's, not only are not hindered by being entities, but *must* be such. They must be I's to be able to address thou's.

My claim is that as long as God is Persuader and thus appropriately sensitive to the needs and rights of all creatures, there is no danger in its being an entity. This is not to say that God is just one entity alongside others, nor that God is one part totalized in an all-embracing whole. Using the same term "entity" of both God and creatures does not take away God's difference from creatures. It allows that what we creatures are in our special, limited ways God is in a unique, perfect way. God is perfect entity, *the* being from which we finite beings originate and to which we contribute our transient but unique and important values.

The suggestion that God is Verb rather than Noun is helpful in that it highlights the dynamism and development that must be kept at the heart of our concept of God. However, it can be misleading. It may suggest that in order to escape a static God, we must go to a Reality without ontological structure and enduring identity. I am not alleging that Daly asserts this. We have already seen that she speaks of God as Be-ing, an active mode which both is, and is not yet; and we have noted her important doctrine of unfolding, which clearly requires that God be more than structureless flux. An unfolding God must contain a reservoir of potentialities and an accumulation of realized actualities. In Whitehead's language, God must have both "primordial" and "consequent" natures. If God is to be perfected and enriched by humanity's "active belief," however (as Daly suggests, agreeing with William James, A. N. Whitehead, and Charles Hartshorne), God must be not only Action (Verb) but also the enduring Substance

(Noun) which receives and preserves these human contributions.[21]

4. REASONABLE BELIEF

We have now stood before the four faces of absurdity and considered what these imposing negativities mean for those who wish to believe in God without closing their eyes to reality. Abandonment: to some it seems that we have all been left to wander in the trackless immensity of space, down an endless spiral of time. Betrayal: to some it seems God has delivered its own people into the hands of pagan murderers. Hatred: to some it seems God has singled out their racial group as the special target of its contempt. Suppression: to more than half the human race it seems God will not or cannot prevent one sex from inhibiting and brutalizing the other.

We have gazed at these irrationalities and asked whether they can be overcome. Is it possible to break through our isolation and sense God's presence in nature? Is it possible to explain how genocide can occur in a world governed by a just and compassionate God? Is it possible to reconcile racial and sexual oppression with a God who is supposed to love all kinds of people equally? We have ventured to answer yes and have offered some reasons why a positive response is justified. How plausible these reasons are, others must judge.

Let us be clear, however, about what I have been attempting to do. I have not tried to prove that my position is *the* truth because I do not think that any cosmology can be established as the only plausible view for everyone. Instead, I have sought the more limited goal of removing the sting of inconsistency from my own version of the God of history. I have tried to show (1) that the loneliness and mortality of human beings in this vast universe do not necessarily imply that God is either hostile or nonexistent and (2) that the diabolical cruelty which some human beings inflict on others because of religious, racial, or sexual bigotry does not necessarily imply that God is either indifferent or malevolent. I have tried to break the logical hold of absurdity and show that one can believe in a God who is benevolent, wise, just, and adequately powerful—without falling into irrationality.

Admittedly, this program will appeal chiefly to those who already believe in God. I said from the start that I would proceed as one who is committed to God as a personal existent who transcends the world and participates by power and persuasion in human affairs and the processes of nature. I reaffirm this now. I believe in this God and am resolved to continue doing so. I think it artificial and self-deceiving to promise to suspend belief in order to consider the issues with innocent eyes. No true believer can be coolly disinterested in the outcome of such a momentous inquiry.

At the same time, neither am I a pure partisan. A competent theologian cannot be. Those who believe in God recognize their own finitude and know that they are vulnerable to error in all matters—theological matters especially. Part of what believing in God means is that, concerning God, we see as in a glass, darkly. Paradoxically, the very belief in God which predisposes us to think that we discern a God at work in the world also keeps us open to correction and possible refutation. We cannot really believe in God without doubting God, without acknowledging that our belief may be mistaken.

Although our discussion will be useful mostly to those who already believe, it is not without importance to others. If the occurrence of great evil is not incompatible with the benevolence of God, this should be set forth for all to hear. All persons, whatever their personal commitments, need to consider the case for the reasonableness of belief. Those who intend to continue rejecting God can do so with a clearer notion of why they hold back, and those who wish to commence believing can make their move with greater understanding of what they are committing themselves to. Even if proof is not possible, persuasion to new or more deeply held commitments is. I can only hope that the discussion has contributed to this end and in some way lessened the attitudes of racial, religious, and sexist hatred which now deaden our hearts to the invitations of the Heavenly Parent who would lead us and go with us from slavery to liberty.

CHAPTER 5

HUMAN COWARDICE
&
DIVINE IMPOTENCE

Although I am persuaded that the view I have been presenting is sound, I am aware that it is open to several serious criticisms. Before I can rest my case, I must face the two most troublesome of these—the contentions that (1) belief in God is an act of cowardice, and (2) a powerless God is inadequate to the world's needs.

1. THE COWARDICE OF THE BELIEVER

This is what Camus is getting at when he says of Kierkegaard's leap of faith: "The leap does not represent an extreme danger as Kierkegaard would like it to do. The danger, on the contrary, lies in the subtle instant that precedes the leap. Being able to remain on that dizzying crest—that is integrity and the rest is subterfuge."[1] Enduring the perpetual frustration and disappointment of absurdity—that is courage. This is precisely what believers fail to do. Instead of facing the world as it is, they anesthetize themselves with fantasies of a world to come. Compared with Sisyphus, who bears his agony like an adult, believers are like frightened children.

Camus makes this charge not only against believers like Kierkegaard, who commit themselves to a personal God, but even against other philosophers who do no more than affirm some philosophic first principle. Husserl, Heidegger, Jaspers, for example, all arbitrarily postulate an absolute principle of intelligibility or being which rescues them from absurdity.[2] They fail to remain true to what they know. They *know* the absurdity of humanity's plight—indeed, they are justly famed for their discerning descriptions of it—yet they do not display the courage necessary to remain faithful to it. They commit "philosophical suicide."[3]

As a model of courage Camus gives us Sisyphus, the mythical king of Corinth, "wisest and most prudent of the mortals." As Camus retells the myth, Sisyphus is punished for treating the gods with levity and stealing their secrets. Sisyphus hated death and loved "this world, enjoyed water and warm stones and the sea." For his defiance he is imprisoned in Hades, condemned forever to push a rock uphill only to have it thunder back to the bottom upon reaching the summit. For a lesser man this perpetual futility would be torture beyond endurance, but to Sisyphus it is a stimulus to greatness. We see it, says Camus, each time the stone hurtles back to the plain. "It is during that return, that pause, that Sisyphus interests me. . . . At each of those moments he leaves the heights and gradually sinks toward the lair of the gods he is superior to his fate. He is stronger than his rock." Instead of despairing, Sisyphus understands his situation and accepts it, and in so doing he attains a grandeur which makes him not only superior to his fate and stronger than his rock, but (I think Camus is saying) nobler than the gods. For all his suffering, Sisyphus is happy.[4]

One reason for the charge of cowardice is that on the surface, belief seems facile. Consider the alternatives which face the person deciding between belief and unbelief. To believe in God is to see oneself within the safety of a universe which is governed by a compassionate, all-powerful Creator, while to decline to believe is to see oneself carried along blindly by galactic tides which care nothing for human beings. Obviously, the former is vastly easier to accept. In a God-tended world one has a well-defined place, a purpose, and a protector; one is a person of worth; and one can rely on God to guarantee a triumphant outcome. The God-less world, by contrast, offers only laceration, despair, and loneliness.

Viewed in this light, does not the character of the absurdist have greater appeal? We naturally admire those who stand on their own feet and tackle their problems without asking for help. Such persons strike us as realistic and resourceful. Moreover, because in their universe the opposition is so formidable and the dangers so great, our sympathies go out to them. If they fight well and endure, if they ask no quarter, we want to praise them: Sisyphus, the wisest and best of mortals! What do we feel for believers except envy at their good fortune and perhaps contempt for their inability to stand up to the world alone?

Surely this unflattering comparison represents only the most superficial reading of motives. A fully sensitive consideration reveals something far different. For one thing, believers do not have the comfort of knowing that their protector exists. Although they sometimes say that they do ("I know that my redeemer liveth!"), actually what they mean by "know" is: "deeply feel that," "am firmly convinced that," or "am willing to risk my life for," all of which are rhetorical ways of saying "believe in." Believers, as I see them, have no evidence strong enough to eliminate doubt and risk.

It is true that some theists claim more than this. A few maintain that the existence of God can be proved logically, and many more think that religious experience yields indubitable intuitive knowledge of God. I think that these claims are unconvincing. In the case of proving God by logic: even if the arguments are valid—and philosophers still disagree on whether they are—they do not prove the God of religion, the conscious, compassionate God of the Bible, Koran, or Bhagavad-Gita. At most, they prove only what David Hume said—that there is a first cause bearing perhaps some resemblance to human intelligence.[5]

In the case of intuitive knowledge religious experience does more to create uncertainty than to remove it. Prayer and mystic contemplation are intrinsically private and therefore unverifiable. No one can directly inspect another's consciousness. Moreover, since religious experience consists of a relation to the absolutely unique and transcendent, it is essentially mysterious. Mystics are convinced that something overwhelmingly significant has happened to them, but they cannot *know* whether it is God they have encountered—much less whether their images and verbal descriptions truly represent the reality disclosed there.

Thus, although some believers claim to be rationally certain of God's existence, actually they are not. They live without proof. To believe in God is to venture into the unknown, to leave security behind; and this, surely, has an important bearing on our question. Cowards do not readily make highly important, dangerous moves without evidence that they will be safe. The decision about whether to believe in God is not merely a crucial question; it is the most important decision a human being can make. It determines the basic character of one's entire life, on earth and beyond. I submit that the decision to believe in God, if made thoughtfully and unreservedly, requires as much fortitude as any decision one is capable of. If one is wrong and there is no God, after all, the direction of one's entire life has been fundamentally mistaken. One has erred on the most important issue of all, the question of what human life is about and the spiritual qualities by which life is best organized and conducted. If there is no God, the believer has, "like the donkey, fed on the roses of illusion." By comparison, Camus's "absurd man" is securely placed. Although he knows little, what he knows he grasps with certainty; and what he knows locates him clearly in the scheme of things and gives him the first principles of his ethics. He is as securely anchored as any believer in God.

Moreover, believers bear a special hardship. They suffer not only the evils of existence which all humans suffer but the anxiety of knowing that these very evils also count against their religious beliefs. Every evil is both a pain to be borne and an item of *prima facie* evidence that humankind's deepest beliefs are illusory. There is no way to avoid this double jeopardy, for believers can neither ignore the evils before their eyes nor deny the belief that all things are providentially ordered. As believers, they are committed to the proposition that God is at work keeping peace and maintaining bonds of mutual concern which are deeper and more lasting than the obvious forces of dissension. For the Christian, at least, this is not a mere hope, but an affirmation of present truth. In Christ, God *has* overcome meaninglessness, removed guilt, conquered death.

The problem, of course, is that much of the evidence available in everyday life is either neutral or seemingly contradictory to this. Millions of human beings exist without meaningful goals, live without forgiveness for their transgressions, and die without expectation of survival. To say that for them there *is* redeeming purpose, forgiveness, and eternal life seems not only mistaken but foolish. Those who have experienced the incredulous and patronizing gaze of friends who do not share their belief that God is at hand moderating the pains and disharmonies of the world know how naïve their beliefs seem to many others whose judgments they respect. The point here is simply that believers carry burdens which are not often noticed: their hopes are as heavy as Sisyphus' despair and require as much courage to sustain.

This is not to say that all believers are courageous and never commit themselves out of cowardice or other low motives. Surely they do. Where there is so much to be gained, greed springs up easily. The logic of Pascal's "wager" is an excellent example of belief that arises from venal motives: "Do you doubt that God exists and that there is eternal life? Go ahead and believe, anyway," invites Pascal. "Act as if you believed whether you do or not. Wager that it is so. What is there to lose? If you guess right, you gain an eternity of happiness, and if you guess wrong, you lose nothing that you would not lose anyhow."[6] It is just such thinking that gives religious belief the reputation of being the easy way out, and unfortunately multitudes have understood their commitments in a similar way.

Surely, however, Pascal is dangerously mistaken. It is not true that believers lose nothing. What of integrity? If we falsely say that we believe and go through the motions of belief, our attitudes and behavior will forever be stained by this self-serving duplicity. What Pascal fails to point out is that the stakes are greater than merely winning or losing eternity, whatever that means. There is also the quality of life of persons here and now and—should there be a future life—forever. Those who act insincerely on beliefs which they think are untrue adopt a certain way of life. They alter their way of thinking and feeling, their treatment of other persons, their expectations of the future. What is at stake is what persons are to become, and that is determined as much by how and why they choose as by what. A paradox awaits us. If we win the wager, having believed out of self-aggrandizing motives, we prove ourselves unworthy of the reward and we lose. Furthermore, if the wager is lost, that is, if God does not exist, we lose not only eternity but the simple enjoyment of the present. We trade common sense for groundless fancies. In our shrewdness we lose our own souls.

Actually, I think, what Pascal urges is not true religious belief. Persons who believe in God because it seems a profitable thing to do are by definition not really believing in God. They are looking for gain, seeking security, or fleeing from emptiness and the terror of extinction. This motive will never win. Even if they are lucky and win their fifty-fifty bet, they fail spiritually, for they do not give *themselves*. They calculate odds and lay chips on the table, but they do not risk themselves.

A reply might be made that this is not a serious problem, because we can never know whether we are mistaken about God. Verification of religious beliefs is "eschatological," that is, possible only at the end of time. If God does not exist, we shall never know it, since when we die we shall simply perish. On this hypothesis it seems believers have the advantage. If God does exist, then after death they will learn of it and enjoy the reward for their fidelity; and if God does not exist, then like everyone else they will simply cease to be. In either case, they will have no regrets.

This is not convincing, however. For one thing, it is conceivable that even without God there is a continuation of consciousness after death. If so, the wasted opportunities and misdirected energies of a believing life could haunt us forever. Moreover, even if death brings instant and final annihilation of all sentience, believers have a *present* knowledge that they may be quite wrong. They live constantly in the realization that there is an even chance that they have fantastically deluded themselves. If they are honest, they know that they live suspended between hope and despair. The point is that persons who take a positive stand on the question of God take risks and expose themselves to error and futility. Done thoughtfully, believing in God is not the move for cowards.

Another reason that belief is sometimes regarded as cowardice is the thought—hardened, since Freud, into an axiom—that believing in God is mere wish fulfillment. When children are too old to depend any longer upon the protection of their biological father, but have not developed the courage to face the unknown by themselves, they project a heavenly father. Thus, belief is a delusion generated by the immature ego to protect itself from the harsh reality of a world which is, in fact, without special regard for human beings. This psychic maneuvering goes on unconsciously, almost automatically, in all but the most mature and disciplined persons. At some stage everyone goes through this neurosis. Some overcome it and achieve adulthood; others remain perpetual adolescents.

Although Freud's theories on religion have by no means been accepted universally, they have given focus to widely felt suspicions and put belief in a most vulnerable position. No thoughtful persons today can be oblivious to the fact that their religious beliefs, complete with assurances of personal worth and promises of eventual fulfillment, conform suspiciously closely to their desires. We cannot help but wonder. Are these desires for heavenly support healthy needs, or are they symptoms of emotional retardation? Do believers permit fantasies to distort their concept of reality? Do they hold themselves back from a fully adult level of life? This kind of questioning haunts every thoughtful believer.

The fact that it does haunt thoughtful believers makes a decisive difference, for once believers become conscious of the so-called neurotic origins of their early inclination to believe and of their present inclination to continue to believe, believing becomes vastly more difficult. They see that there are indeed people who believe in God very much the way Freud says, and that they may be among them. They know how easy it is to believe what they wish to believe and to accept simple, consoling answers—especially when the answers cannot be disproved. They know how adept human beings are at deceiving themselves and others. Nevertheless, in full awareness of the suspicions they are likely to arouse in others, they elect to believe. Can we say of such persons that they are obviously moved basically by fear and weakness?

Let us go beyond this. Suppose we master our self-doubts and enter an active relationship of belief. Now for a time the uncertainty subsides. We do not agonize over whether any divine reality corresponds to our belief, and we are not paralyzed by fears that in thinking this is so we are indulging our puerile desires. Have we now reached a plateau where belief is safe and pleasant? In a sense this is true. A maturing spiritual life does give serenity. Think of Kierkegaard's prayers and discourses, written in the "religious" stage of his life. The sense of peace and trust expressed there, when contrasted with the sense of conflict and struggle in the earlier "ethical" and "aesthetic" stages, illustrates how belief can develop and yield tangible psychic satisfactions. Still this does not indicate that belief becomes easy. The old difficulties will disappear only to be replaced by different ones. It was in Kierkegaard's last and presumably most mature phase that he wrote the melancholic thought, "Those whom God loves he makes to suffer."[7] The questioning stage of belief is followed by an acting stage in which one works to carry out the implications of belief. This is, if anything, more difficult than the initial stage. Genuine belief is never a cozy repose in the almighty arms.

As Rudolph Otto and many other students of religious

experience have documented, to be in the presence of the Creator is an awesome thing. True religion begins in the fear of God, says Buber. God is not only the "ground of being," Tillich asserts, but also the "abyss." God is not just the source and support of all that exists, but also that which ultimately opposes and threatens. "Infinity," "absoluteness," "holiness," "judge"—these attributes point to that quality of God which disturbs and confounds us. To *believe* in this being—not merely to profess or think about it—is to open up, reach out, respond, and encounter; and this is anything but tranquil. Serious intercourse with the divine may be so upsetting that by comparison, living in a godless world is a pleasant respite.

Ethically, too, belief poses problems. Believers are faced not only by whatever ethical standard fits the situation they face, but also by the Holy One from whom the standard derives. God not only gives the law but commands us to obey it; God lays a claim upon each individual to act: to do this deed, here, now. The God of religion is active goodness. Its nature is to be constantly sponsoring what is good. God establishes the possibilities and conditions for enhancing what already exists, and, also, for introducing fresh goods; moreover, God interacts with those creatures who are capable of rational choice, striving to persuade them to join in the venture. To believing persons, the world is a portentous cosmic drama. In some ways it is tragic, in some ways joyous; but always it is full of potential meaning. Of course, I am not asserting that all who say they are believers constantly conceive of their lives in these terms and constantly live under such supreme pressure. As T. S. Eliot cautions in *Four Quartets*, "humankind cannot bear very much reality."[8] However, whenever believers take their own world view seriously, and open their consciousness fully to what it entails, they find themselves having to

112

choose in a context which is charged with significance and difficulty. God confronts us with dreadful alternatives and scarcely endurable conflicts. Shall we choose light or darkness, life or death, fulfillment or frustration? God asks that we give ourselves without reservation and allows us but a brief lifetime to respond. God holds us to a standard of absolute perfection and warns us to be satisfied with nothing less. God places on us a burden of responsibility which few can carry completely and none can carry alone. Unceasing in its persuasion toward good, God compels us to shape our own destiny.

Of course, there are also positive, rewarding aspects to the believer's situation; but at the moment, in order to make the point, I wish to highlight the arduous ones. Believers live not only under self-imposed standards and social conventions which they can alter or ignore with relative impunity, but under independent, universal standards which make a claim upon them irrespective of human preference. "Condemned to be free," Sartre says of humanity. Believers in God must also say this of themselves, and more. They are also "called to be responsible." And not in Sartre's flamboyant manner—that is, "in anguish" because each of us legislates for all humanity— but under God, showing responsibility for this person here, now, in God's special, caring way. Believing persons must not only assume responsibility and decide what to do, they must also do these things in relation to an absolute standard which they must discern, translate, accept, and apply.

Added to all of this is the further difficulty that belief must be constantly repeated. Some critics apparently think that belief involves a single leap. Believers, it would appear, have only to reach the desperation point, the "boundary situation," where they cease thinking, turn their backs on common sense, utter one final mindless cry of submission, and ever thereafter live in smug imperviousness to doubt.

This is a gross misunderstanding. All who have seriously wrestled with belief and unbelief and tried conscientiously to make their own commitment know that the leap of belief must be constantly repeated. In one respect, "leap" is a poor metaphor since it implies that the leaper's feet soon touch solid ground, which is not so. Perhaps "flight" would be a better image. A bird flying or a fish swimming, at once buoyed by a fluid and propelled by its own efforts, suggests the continuity and repeated movement of belief. We "let go" of our frightened dependence on proximate certainties and break out of the cramped system in which we have found security. We detach ourselves and begin moving in new ways. Whatever the analogy, genuine belief in God involves "dreadful," constant, lifelong exertion. To begin to believe is to begin to be a self, to dare to act as an eternal spirit.

In addition, the life of belief is subject to the usual problems which all persons face. Believers are not exempt from the ordinary human difficulties and sorrows. They must still work for their bread and endure the slow shipwreck of their psychophysical selves. They too worry about their children, grieve for those who suffer, regret their personal perfidies, and sorrow over the despoliation of the planet. They too become ill and die.

In fact, those who choose to believe should feel the ills of the world with special poignancy, since their God is involved in the creation. God is creating the world, providing for its sustenance, working to mend its flaws and follies, enjoying its achievements. All who follow this God must also be involved with the world and with God's involvement with it; they must love what God loves, hate what God hates. God's pain augments their pain just as God's joy augments their joy. For believers, everything is intensified. Every peak is higher, every depression deeper.

There is initial plausibility about this move. Does not the absurd one by refusing to reach out hopefully show a lack of nerve? Camus has got it right that this is the crucial moment, but he seems to have erred in thinking that unbelief is more demanding. Does not Sisyphus choose the easier way? Does he not hold on to what is certain—his intuition of absurdity—and does he not thereby turn absurdity into an absolute and thus do precisely what Camus reproaches the other existentialists for? Has he not, like them, given the world a specious intelligibility as a place of moral testing?

This might be argued convincingly, I think. Let us pursue it for a moment. If Camus and other absurdists are right, the human situation offers several certainties. We *know* that we are alone in the world and that all of our constructive efforts must at last come to nought. We *know* that there is no escape and that every tomorrow will be like today. Absurdity guarantees our future. As surely as the sun rises, our stone will roll back down the slope and we shall have to begin again, profoundly frustrated, to be sure, but ennobled by our own honesty and perseverance.

Believers, by contrast, have no such assurance. They push their rock continuously without receiving palpable signals as to their progress. Sometimes it seems that they move ahead, sometimes that they fall back. They struggle toward what they assume is the top, without even knowing whether there is a top. Actually, the struggle of those who seek to believe calls for a different metaphor, something less circumscribed than the Sisyphus and boulder image. Believing in God is more like a journey through unknown terrain to an uncertain destination. It is the uncertainty that is most troublesome. Is it possible that believers are, as they hope, moving toward a joyful arrival? Is there a destination at all? Believers are troubled not only as Sisyphus is, with the suffering along the way, but also with anxiety that perhaps the journey leads nowhere except to annihilation and that they are playing the fool by living otherwise. In short, believers are subject to some pressures which nonbelievers are spared.

Shall we then conclude that belief is categorically more courageous than disbelief? The argument seems to lead there, and I am bound to say so. There do seem to be crucial differences between the life based on belief in God and the life based on absurdity, and the two lives do not seem equally true and efficacious. Camus and Buber see different meanings in their common world: the first sees absurdity; the second, the Eternal Thou. And Camus and Kierkegaard have radically diverse expectations about what awaits us at the end of life: Camus, annihilation; Kierkegaard, eternal society (heaven). Believers and unbelievers may agree on many ethical principles and practical policies, and they may be colleagues and friends; but they still have very different notions of the human situation, of what we should do to find meaning, and of how we are to relate personally to others. Camus's outlook is happiness rooted in despair; Kierkegaard's is sadness rooted in hope; and I have no doubt that I find Kierkegaard's outlook closer to the truth.[9]

However, I am uneasy about making this claim, not only because it sounds pompous, but because it may very well be mistaken. It is very easy to misunderstand and underrate a rival point of view. No doubt I have overlooked some aspects of Camus's life of humanistic independence which make its defenders think it superbly strong and honorable. Mostly I have treated this redoubtable alternative in terms of its negative features, particularly that it denies God and purpose. However, it also has many positive features. Camus is committed to humanity, life, truth, integrity; Sartre to freedom; Bertrand Russell to truth and justice;

William R. Jones to the liberation of the oppressed; Alistair Kee to the life of transcendence. Do not these lofty ideals place as severe a demand on their devotees as God does upon the believer?

We must face the fact that human beings just do differ in their basic perceptions of reality, and it is very difficult to say that one set of perceptions is nobler than another. On the question of whether the world is derived from God, equally perceptive persons see different patterns. Behind our common human sufferings Camus sees absurdity, Kierkegaard sees Providence. They see differently not because one suffers greatly and the other does not, but because they expect different things from life, make different assumptions about what is possible, and read the evidence different ways. Camus derives suffering from irrationality, Kierkegaard links it with paradoxical love. The first defines despair as virtue and chooses to remain in it; the latter defines despair as sin and tries to transcend it.

Since I cannot see into the hearts of others, I must assume that there can be as much integrity and spiritual strength within those who do not believe as within those who do. As Kierkegaard teaches in his doctrine of truth as subjectivity, what makes a religious affirmation "true" (effective in relating one to God) is not that it objectively pictures the facts, but that it is held with total passion and sincerity. Theological statements, unlike any other kind, can be objectively false but subjectively true.[10]

I do not take the same mischievous delight in this paradox that Kierkegaard does, but I do see how our inescapable uncertainty about God puts a high value on courage and how it might make every "ultimately concerned" decision, whether it issues in belief or disbelief, precious in the eyes of God. Thus, I shall not assert the supremacy of belief over disbelief, but shall be satisfied if what has been said on behalf of belief has blunted the charge of cowardice and established that believing in God can be a strong and positive way of living.

2. DIVINE IMPOTENCE

The second criticism the doctrine of a persuading God must face is that an impotent God cannot do for the world what it needs to have done and therefore is no God at all. If God cannot control the destructive parts of the creation, humanity may never be able to throw off oppression, never begin to compensate for the horrors of the past, never escape the paralyzing threat of catastrophic destruction. A God powerless to prevent diabolic destruction cannot guarantee even the *survival* of its creatures, much less their happiness and fulfillment. With such a God the ancient dream of the coming kingdom of God turns into a nightmare of perpetual frustration and defeat, a veritable hell on earth.

Does the idea of a God limited in power carry such disastrous implications? Clearly, the answer to this depends on how much we think human beings can do and endure. How much deprivation can we stand? What must we be *given* in order to become fully human? Must we be absolutely protected against disaster—*guaranteed* life, liberty, and happiness? Is a God who cannot do this no proper God?

It seems to me that human beings can manage well enough without supernatural guarantees. In fact, we do so. Every moment of our existence is filled with profound danger. Our vital supplies of air, water, and food could be cut off or lethally contaminated at any moment; we are never entirely safe from fire, storm, and disease, from thieves and murderers, from mayhem on the freeway, or from nuclear obliteration. These real possibilities threaten all of us, and they strike some of us irrespective of whether we believe in God. God's rain falls on the just and unjust. Although believers hold that God will eventually turn all evil to good and that they will taste this good, they do not assume that in the meantime they will suffer less than those who do not believe in God. The point is this: the security we have is sufficient. As human beings we are tough, and we do not have to be entirely shielded from tragedy. We are capable of preventing many of the evils which befall us, and we can bear those we cannot prevent.

Even so, the critics among us are not likely to be satisfied. They will say that human resilience and fortitude are all very well, but what we need is to be assured that we shall not be overwhelmed by destructivity and that we *can* do something to make the world at least a little better. For this we need a God who possesses real power and can keep evil within reasonable bounds, who can arouse and facilitate human creativity and guarantee that when human beings have done all they can do to resist evil, their efforts will be supported and preserved. A persuading God must be able to succeed in its persuasion.

Do we have reason to think that God does succeed in this end? I contend that if we think of God's persuasion as active participation in the world, we will have all the assurance of its potency that we need. Think of God not just as defeated and blocked by the various manifestations of absurdity, but as actively attempting to overcome them. Imagine God as positioned in the center of the world's radical evils, working from within to remove them. Push beyond images of a mere brooding Presence, and think of a fellow Sufferer who takes the world's pains into itself. See God's powerlessness not only as an inability to achieve its ends, but also as a voluntarily assumed condition intended to call forth from all rational creatures the very actions which they must take to become God's co-creators. See powerlessness as a fulcrum

119

by which human beings can become more powerful than they otherwise would be. Visualize divine powerlessness in its paradoxicality—as the potency of persuasion. In this we can find the guarantee we need—not that we *shall* overcome, but that with God's sustenance, we *can.*

There are various ways to represent this redemptive divine suffering, including the classical images of Gautama as Bodhissatva, Israel as Suffering Servant, and Jesus as Crucified Messiah; but these traditional forms speak less compellingly today than others which more graphically display the complete innocence and helplessness of the victim. I am thinking of the brutalized children depicted in Dostoevsky's, Camus's, and Elie Wiesel's fiction. Think of Ivan Karamazov's impassioned protest to Alyosha on behalf of children abused and battered by their parents. Recall the police magistrate's son in *The Plague,* who dies so agonizingly despite Dr. Rieux's desperate ministrations. Especially think of Elie Wiesel's story of the young Jewish boy who is hanged in the Nazi death camp. The horrified crowd watches as the executioners put the noose around the child's neck. Will the monsters actually execute a child? Desperately, despairingly someone asks "Where is God? Where is He?" No one answers. The order is given and the executioners push the child and his two fellow victims off the chairs on which they stand; the nooses snap taut around the three necks. At that moment, in the mind of the horrified witnesses, an inner voice responds to the old man's unanswered question with: "Where is He? Here He is—He is hanging on this gallows."[11]

Here is an incident more fact than fiction, yet stated in a compelling fictional image. Multiply it by a million to represent all the children murdered in the Holocaust; vary the details to include black children bombed in Alabama or starved in Detroit; extend it to Bangladesh, Nigeria,

Vietnam, or India, and it speaks to our situation with exactitude and trenchancy. Could we not use this idea of joint human-divine suffering as a key by which to understand our situation and God's? Only, of course, if we can believe that God in truth is as powerless and as vulnerable to suffering as the least of its creatures.

Granted, Ivan Karamazov and Dr. Rieux interpret the suffering of their children as implying the absence of God (and they certainly do not present the children as models of divine suffering); it is also true that Ivan and Dr. Rieux—mistakenly, if my argument is correct—think of God as a being who possesses the power to prevent such evils. If we repudiate this kind of power and conceive of God as sharing the situation of all human beings—particularly those who suffer unjustly—the images of suffering children can take on a different meaning. If God feels everything its creatures feel (the agony of those who are victimized, the outrage of helpless bystanders, the shame of indifferent bystanders, even the perverted satisfaction and self-hatred of the sadists), as well as its own infinite sorrow, then we must rethink God's relation to suffering. The problem is no longer why God does not prevent suffering, but why human beings do not refrain from violating each other, and why we do not more powerfully respond to all suffering and work with God to eliminate it. We see that it is not God but we who are inactive in the struggle against absurdity. We gain a new respect for God's power and see that God is doing everything which can possibly be done and all that needs to be done. The onus shifts from God to us. The pressure intensifies. A God who is active and available in the midst of every crisis and present in every tragedy is a God who can change the world. The uncertainty is not whether God is with us and able to overcome our suffering, but whether we will join God in the struggle.

121

NOTES

INTRODUCTION

1. Alistair Kee, *The Way of Transcendence* (Baltimore: Penguin Books, 1971), p. ix.
2. Thomas J. J. Altizer, *The Descent into Hell* (Philadelphia and New York: J. B. Lippincott Co., 1970), p. 26.
3. Andrew M. Greeley, *Unsecular Man* (New York: Delta Books, Dell Publishing Co., 1974), p. 11.
4. Robert Wuthnow and Charles Y. Glock, "The Shifting Focus of Faith," *Psychology Today*, November 1974, p. 132.
5. Alasdair MacIntyre, *Difficulties in Christian Belief* (London: SCM Press, 1959), pp. 16–17.
6. *Ibid.*, p. 34.
7. *Ibid.*, pp. 22–27.
8. *Ibid.*, p. 36.
9. *Ibid.*, p. 41.

CHAPTER 1

1. Jean-Paul Sartre, "Existentialism Is a Humanism," in *Existentialism from Dostoevsky to Sartre*, ed. Walter Kaufman (New York: Meridian Books, 1963), pp. 294, 295.
2. Michael Novak, *The Experience of Nothingness* (New York: Harper Colophon Books, 1971), pp. 12–13.
3. See Langdon Gilkey, *Naming the Whirlwind* (Indianapolis and New York: Bobbs-Merrill, 1969), pp. 31–61 and Gabriel Vahanian, *The Death of God* (New York: George Braziller, 1961), p. xxxii.
4. Carl Becker, *The Heavenly City of the Eighteenth-Century Philosophers* (New Haven: Yale University Press, 1963), p. 15.
5. Antony Flew, *God and Philosophy* (London: Hutchinson and Co., 1966), p. 69.
6. Paul Tillich, *The Courage to Be* (New Haven: Yale University Press, 1957), p. 57.
7. Albert Camus, *The Plague* (New York: Modern Library, 1948), p. 193.

8. *Ibid.*, pp. 196–97.
9. Camus, *The Rebel* (New York: Vintage Books, 1962), p. 24.
10. Camus, *The Plague,* p. 229.
11. Camus, *The Rebel,* pp. 8–12.
12. *Ibid.*, p. 23.
13. Albert Camus, *The Myth of Sisyphus* (New York: Vintage Books, 1961), p. 14.
14. Camus, *The Rebel,* p. 24.
15. *Ibid.*, p. 21.
16. Camus, *The Rebel,* pp. 13–22.
17. Camus, *The Myth of Sisyphus,* pp. 17, 27.
18. *Ibid.*, p. 15.
19. *Ibid.*, p. 14.
20. *Ibid.*, p. 21.
21. *Ibid.*, p. 39.
22. *Ibid.*, p. 13.
23. *Ibid.*, p. 42.
24. John Loose, "The Christian as Camus's Absurd Man," *Journal of Religion,* July 1962, p. 203.
25. *Ibid.*, p. 212.
26. *Ibid.*, p. 213.

CHAPTER 2

1. Alice L. Eckardt, "The Holocaust: Jewish and Christian Responses," *Journal of the American Academy of Religion,* 42 (September 1974), 453.
2. Paul J. Kirsch, *We Christians and Jews* (Philadelphia: The Fortress Press, 1975), p. 66.
3. Emil Fackenheim, Gates Lecture at Grinnell College, 15 October 1972.
4. Richard Rubenstein, *After Auschwitz* (Indianapolis and New York: Bobbs-Merrill, 1966), p. 65.
5. Emil Fackenheim, *God's Presence in History* (New York: Harper Torchbooks, 1972), p. 73.
6. *Ibid.*, p. 74.
7. *Ibid.*, p. 76.
8. *Ibid.*, pp. 77–78.
9. *Ibid.*, p. 78.
10. *Ibid.*, p. 81.
11. *Ibid.*, p. 82.
12. *Ibid.*, p. 83.
13. *Ibid.*, pp. 85–89.
14. *Ibid.*, p. 84.
15. In November of 1973 I wrote Professor Fackenheim and asked him about this point. I suggested that his writings seem to stop short of faith, that it is clear that he thinks that Jews are prohibited from denying God

but not that they are necessarily commanded to believe. Fackenheim replied in December, 1973, that the logic of his view is that Jews are commanded to believe but that psychologically this is virtually impossible for some. There is a "question [of] how much a man of faith can bear without something snapping." I take this to mean that Fackenheim stops short of saying that Jews must believe in God.

16. Michael Wyschogrod, "Faith and the Holocaust," *Judaism*, Summer 1971, p. 288.

17. Fackenheim, *God's Presence in History*, pp. 76, 84–85.

18. *Ibid.*, p. 88.

19. *Ibid.*, p. 25.

20. *Ibid.*, pp. 24–25.

21. *Ibid.*, p. 20.

22. *Ibid.*, p. 21.

23. *Ibid.*, p. 24.

24. Richard Rubenstein, "Some Perspectives on Religious Faith After Auschwitz," in *The German Church Struggle and the Holocaust*, ed. F. H. Littell, Hubert G. Locke (Detroit: Wayne University Press, 1974), p. 262.

25. *Ibid.*

26. Jacob Neusner, "Implications of the Holocaust," *The Journal of Religion*, 53 (July 1973), 303. Neusner says that "the events of 1933–48 constitute one of the decisive moments in the history of Judaism, to be compared in their far-reaching effects with the destruction of the First and Second Temples, 586 B.C. and A.D. 70; the massacre of Rhineland Jewries, 1096; the aftermath of the Black Plague, 1349; the expulsion of the Jews from Spain, 1492; or the Ukrainian massacres of 1648–50." This is to say, that as terrible as Auschwitz was, it was not essentially different from other great tragedies which the Jewish people have endured before.

27. Wyschogrod, "Faith and the Holocaust," pp. 292–93.

28. Rubenstein, *After Auschwitz*, pp. 125–26, 230–31.

29. Charles Hartshorne, *The Divine Relativity* (New Haven: Yale University Press, 1967), p. 138.

30. Fackenheim, *God's Presence in History*, p. 77.

31. *Ibid.*, pp. 77–78.

32. Hans Jonas, "The Concept of God After Auschwitz," *Out of the Whirlwind*, ed. A. H. Friedlander (New York: Union of American Hebrew Congregations, 1958), p. 468.

33. Eliezer Berkovits, *Faith After the Holocaust* (New York: KATV Publishing House), p. 105.

34. MacIntyre, *Difficulties in Christian Belief*, p. 36.

35. Berkovits, *Faith After the Holocaust*, p. 109.

36. Ignaz Maybaum, *The Face of God After Auschwitz* (Amsterdam, 1965), p. 32.

37. Elie Wiesel, *The Gates of the Forest* (New York: Avon Books, 1972), pp. 196–97.

CHAPTER 3

1. William R. Jones, *Is God a White Racist?* (Garden City, N. Y.: Doubleday Anchor, 1974), p. 205. Jones says, "I would regard black suffering as more severe than Jewish suffering. Basil Davidson, for instance, estimates that slavery before and after embarkation cost fifty million black souls. . . . Yet numbers alone do not tell the total story. I do not detect decimation of Jewish culture and tradition, but decimation of black culture and tradition characterizes life in America."
2. James Cone, *Black Theology and Black Power* (New York: The Seabury Press, 1969), p. 6.
3. Jones, *Is God a White Racist?* p. 205.
4. *Ibid.*, p. 74.
5. *Ibid.*, p. xiii.
6. Jones to Burkle, 25 May 1975.
7. Jones, *Is God a White Racist?* pp. 7–9.
8. *Ibid.*, p. 10.
9. *Ibid.*, pp. 49–51.
10. *Ibid.*, p. 20.
11. *Ibid.*, p. 29.
12. *Ibid.*, pp. 186–93.
13. *Ibid.*, p. 197.
14. *Ibid.*, p. xii.
15. *Ibid.*, p. 194.
16. *Ibid.*, p. 64.
17. I am not denying that the world *may* be dominated by a power or powers which are indifferent to, remote from, or malevolent toward human beings. I am simply saying that these forces should not be called God, and that the cosmology incorporating such powers should be called atheistic. Neither am I denying that indifference, remoteness, and malevolence are present within a theistic cosmology. Malevolence may be present in a satanic principle that God permits but ultimately controls. Indifference and remoteness toward human beings may be part of nature and thus be present in the human environment, but they must be present for ultimately beneficent reasons—to provide human beings with the distance and independence they need to achieve freedom.
18. Jones, *Is God a White Racist?* p. xv.
19. *Ibid.*, p. 194.
20. *Ibid.*, p. 30.

CHAPTER 4

1. Mary Daly, *Beyond God the Father* (Boston: Beacon Press, 1974), p. 2.
2. *Ibid.*, p. 118.
3. *Ibid.*, p. 13.
4. *Ibid.*

5. *Ibid.*
6. *Ibid.*, p. 15.
7. *Ibid.*, p. 20.
8. *Ibid.*, p. 17.
9. *Ibid.*, pp. 28–29.
10. *Ibid.*, p. 21.
11. *Ibid.*, pp. 30–31.
12. *Ibid.*, p. 21.
13. *Ibid.*, pp. 33–34.
14. *Ibid.*, p. 36.
15. *Ibid.*, p. 37.
16. *Ibid.*, p. 29.
17. *Ibid.*, p. 33.
18. *Ibid.*, p. 40.
19. Elie Wiesel, "Talking and Keeping Silent," in *The German Church Struggle and the Holocaust,* ed. F. H. Littel and Hubert G. Locke (Detroit: Wayne University Press, 1974), p. 271.
20. Daly, *Beyond God the Father,* p. 23.
21. *Ibid.*, p. 37.

CHAPTER 5

1. Albert Camus, *The Myth of Sisyphus* (New York: Vintage Books, 1961), p. 37.
2. *Ibid.*, see pp. 17–21.
3. *Ibid.*, p. 31.
4. *Ibid.*, pp. 89, 91.
5. David Hume, *Dialogues Concerning Natural Religion* (New York: Hafner Publishing Company, 1948), p. 94.
6. Blaise Pascal, "The Heart Has Its Reasons," in *Readings in the Philosophy of Religion,* ed. John A. Mourant (New York: Thomas Y. Crowell, 1956), pp. 26–27.
7. Sören Kierkegaard, *Attack upon Christendom* (Boston: Beacon Press, 1957), p. 157.
8. T. S. Eliot, *Four Quartets* (New York: Harcourt, Brace and Co., 1943), p. 4.
9. Camus seemed to like representing his position in dialectical opposition to Christianity. For instance, in a talk delivered to Christian monks he said "If Christianity is pessimistic as to man, it is optimistic as to human destiny. Well, I can say that, pessimistic as to human destiny, I am optimistic as to man." *Resistance, Rebellion, and Death* (London: Hamish Hamilton, 1961), p. 51.
10. Sören Kierkegaard, *Concluding Unscientific Postscript* (Princeton: Princeton University Press, 1960), p. 178.
11. Elie Wiesel, *Night* (New York: Pyramid Books, 1961), p. 78.

INDEX

Absurdity, "faces" of, 15–16; as abandonment, 19, 22; Camus's doctrine of, 23, 24–25, 30–33; as Christian concept, 36; as genocide, 43; as hatred, 64; as sexism, 88–89; flight from, 103–4; as security, 115
Agnosticism, 72–73
Altizer, Thomas, 13
Atheism, 71, 73, 74, 91

Becker, Carl, 20
Belief, difficulty of, 11, 14, 107–8; among the oppressed, 94, 96–97; rational, 100–102; motives of, 108, 109–11, 119–21; risks of, 105–6, 107, 118–20; burdens of, 113–14; as venture, 115; superiority of, 116–18
Berkovits, Eliezer, 57, 60–61
Black humanism, 71
Bonhoeffer, Dietrich, 19, 22
Buber, Martin, 19, 98, 112, 116

Camus, Albert, 22, 50, 64, 68, 98, 103–4, 107, 115–17, 120
Cleage, Albert, 67
Conceptual analysis, 66
Cone, James, 64
Counterevidence, method of, 76
Cox, Harvey, 22
Cullen, Countee, 71, 72, 78

Daly, Mary, 88
Death, 23–30, 34, 37–42, 47
Deism, 71
Dostoevsky, Fëdor, 120

Eckhardt, Alice, 44
Eliot, T. S., 112
Eschatology, as deliverance, 69–70; as verification, 109
Exaltation event, 84

Fackenheim, Emil, 44, 95

Femaleness, 90, 96
Functional ultimacy, 67, 74, 75

Glock, Charles, 14
God, personal, 11, 12, 94, 98–99; traditional, 11, 51, 89; parental, 12; omnipotence, 17, 35, 52–54, 56–57, 77, 83–85, 121; historical, 45; commanding Voice, 47–48; transcendence, 51, 91, 94; truth, 52; sovereignty, 53, 67; worship-worthiness, 53, 78; perfection, 54, 77, 78, 97; powerlessness, 54–57, 60, 79–80, 83–84, 97, 118–21; eternity, 58; benevolence, 65, 70, 76–77; malevolence, 65, 70–71, 77; responsibility for evil, 59–60, 62, 79; omniscience, 60; freedom, 60; indifference, 77; persuasion, 80, 82–83, 97–98, 119–20; the father, 89–92, 96, 98; substantiality, 92, 99; creativity, 93, 96, 113; suffering, 120–21

Hartshorne, Charles, 12, 54, 99
Hegel, G. W. F., 35
Heidegger, Martin, 103
Holocaust, intelligibility of, 52; as churban, 62
Humanity, creativity of, 61–62; dependence of, 81; freedom of, 61, 79–80, 84–86, 92–93
Hume, David, 106

Idolatry, male, 12
Internal criticism, 66

James, William, 94, 99
Jaspers, Karl, 103
Jonas, Hans, 56
Jones, Major, 67
Jones, William R., 64, 94, 95, 117

Karamazov, Ivan, 120, 121

127